THE SEPTEMBER 11 TERRORIST ATTACKS AND THE INVASION OF IRAQ IN CONTEMPORARY INTERNATIONAL LAW

NIJHOFF LAW SPECIALS

VOLUME 61

The titles published in this series are listed at the end of this volume.

The September 11 Terrorist Attacks and the Invasion of Iraq in Contemporary International Law

Opinions on the Emerging New World Order System

by:
Edward McWhinney, Q.C.

Barrister-at-Law, Barrister and Solicitor,
Professor (em.) of International and Constitutional Law,
Member and President (1999-2001) of *Institut de Droit International*,
sometime Member of the Permanent Court of Arbitration,
sometime Member of Parliament and Parliamentary Secretary
(Foreign Affairs)

MARTINUS NIJHOFF PUBLISHERS
LEIDEN/BOSTON

A C.I.P. Catalogue record for this book is available from the Library of Congress.

Printed on acid-free paper.

ISBN 90-04-14143-X

Brill Academic Publishers incorporates the imprint Martinus Nijhoff Publishers.
http://www.brill.nl

Printed and bound in The Netherlands

CONTENTS

ACKNOWLEDGEMENTS

In the aftermath of the September 11, 2001 events the author was involved in the continuing "great debate", in various international and also national legal arenas, as to the legal foundations of the US and British armed intervention in Iraq, entered upon on March 20, 2003, after the two invading states had signally failed to build majority support in the United Nations Security Council for a draft Resolution that would effectively dispense them from the UN Charter prohibitions on the Use-of-Force. Although the political and political-military developments from the September 11 events on to the Iraq invasion and beyond are properly viewed historically as a *factual* continuum, in terms of the claims involved by the key players, there cannot be said to be any *legal* continuum. There are, rather, differing legal arguments, advanced at different times, while the political problem-situation unfolded as complex and polycentric – a series of separate, not necessarily related political sub-problems, concerning whose basic characterisation and also definition of the controls or remedies available for solution there might be significant differences of opinion. For analytical purposes the problem-situation may better be broken down into three different phases or parts, conveniently falling into three successive time periods:

i. a first phase – international terrorism, *stricto sensu*, narrowly defined and with its own appropriate, recently established international legal controls;
ii. a second phase, in which the problem-definition is widened to involve "rogue states" asserted to be sponsoring or otherwise in collusion with the perpetrators of the September 11 attacks, and with the range of sort-for legal controls correspondingly broadened

to include direct action – pre-emptive military strikes – against the state actors so designated;

iii. a third phase, after the U.S./British invasion in which the focus shifts to the legal foundations for unilateral military action without prior Security Council or General Assembly Resolution explicitly dispensing from the UN Charter prohibitions on the Use-of-Force, and armed Interventions; and with incidental attention to follow-up issues of the legal rights and duties inherent in Belligerent Occupation.

The succeeding publication flows from separate legal studies undertaken by the author in relation to each of the three successive phases outlined above, and prepared and published in March, 2002; October, 2002; and August, 2003 respectively. The opinions are rooted in the political space-time dimension in which they were first made and in the particular fact-complex then existing – either facts of general public knowledge of which judicial notice might properly be taken, or else, less than that, factual scenarios advanced by the principal protagonists in support of their own particular claims, legal as well as political. For almost all the legal claims are dependent, for their successful invocation, upon demonstration and vindication of the factual premises upon which their use is predicated. In phase two, in particular, and the attempted broadening of the definition of the problem-situation to include application of armed force legal controls against claimed "rogue states", the *rôle* of the United Nations' own specially-appointed fact-finding agency, UNMOVIC, in ruling on the continued existence or present non-existence of Weapons of Mass Destruction (WMD) in Iraq becomes the subject of the crucial joinder-of-issue in the UN Security Council debates in February-March, 2003.

Access to facts, disputed facts, and the rendering of definitive judgements on these facts as pre-conditions to legally-based action have been facilitated, retrospectively, by the unusually early publication of memoirs and recollections of former government advisors and assistants who were privy to some of the key decisions of principal political players. The final word on these revelations from within the system, and their accuracy and fairness, must perhaps rest on the reports of official enquiries, legislative and judicial, under way in the main protagonist states involved in the Iraq invasion.

At the price of some inevitable repetition of legal arguments and citations earlier advanced, I am releasing my earlier legal opinions essentially in the form in which they were first developed and written and published, reflecting the then known "truths" of their own distinct time periods and the factual premises on which these "truths" were based. This has been done in respect of Chapters 2, 3 and 4, which contain the original legal opinions with indication of their respective dates of publication, accompanied by extended explanatory head-notes in each case. It is left to the final study, Chapter 5, to essay any necessary corrections or modifications in the hypotheses or conclusions first put forward, in the light of new factual information now available.

I am indebted to the new *Chinese Journal of International Law* (Editor-in-Chief, Professor Sienho Yee, currently of the Faculty of Law of the University of Colorado at Boulder), for permission to use, for the present volume, material previously published in the *Journal* (volumes 1 and 2, (2002) and (2003)). I have felt free to draw, for purposes of present publication, on a note contributed to the *Institut de Droit International*'s 10th Commission (1999-2003) (Thomas Franck, *rapporteur*; subject: the authority under International Law of International Organizations other than the United Nations to use Force); and on lectures to the Institute of Public International Law and International Relations in Thessaloniki in September, 2003 (subject: State Responsibility and the International Law Commission's final Draft Report), which are to be published in that Institut's *Thesaurus Acroasium* (Kalliopi Koufa, Editor). In a guest editorial specially commissioned by the Canadian Council on International Law for its *Bulletin* (volume 29, 2003) I referred to then Canadian Prime Minister, Jean Chrétien, and his position on the UN Charter and the Non-Use-of-Force in the Iraq crisis, and this is drawn on in Chapter 4, part IV. Opinions expressed in the present volume are, of course, those of the author personally and do not engage any of the institutions, private or public, of which the author has been a member in recent years, or any of the public personalities with whom he has been associated during that same time period.

May, 2004

CHAPTER ONE

"LINKAGE" IN INTERNATIONAL LAW. FROM SEPTEMBER 11, 2001 TERRORIST ATTACKS TO MARCH 20, 2003 US/BRITISH INVASION OF IRAQ

In an editorial published on April 9, 2004, a year after the US/British 26-day Blitzkrieg against Iraq ended in its direct military combat phase and President George W. Bush had made his triumphant "Mission accomplished" declaration, the *New York Times* commented:

> The president and his top foreign policy advisors came into office [on January 20, 2001] determined to build a military defense shield, fixated on Iraq as the top problem in the Middle East and greatly concerned about China.

The *New York Times* editors concluded with the wry, succinct judgment:

> [The president] guessed wrong about what deserved the administration's most immediate and intense attention.

In spite of advance warnings from U.S. national security services, it now seems clear from the published revelations of the principal anti-terrorist expert of the Bush administration (and of the Clinton administration before that), Richard Clarke, that the president and his National Security Council head and also his main Cabinet Ministers were all caught by surprise and unprepared for the attacks, mounted on September 11, 2001, through commercial passenger aircraft specially hijacked for that purpose, against the twin World Trade Towers in New York City and the Defence Department's Pentagon building in Washington, D.C. Immediately after those attacks, however, when President Bush announced his determination to track down the perpetrators and planners of the attacks, which were quickly identified, by the admission of its leader, Osama bin Laden, as the work of the al-Qaeda terrorist organization, there was an impressive, widespread rallying of support to the United States administration from member-states of the World Community, strongly reminiscent of the 30-plus states who had joined in the "coalition of the willing", under U.S. military leadership and with the full legal sanction and prior authority of the United Nations, in the Gulf War operations against Iraq in 1990-1. On that occasion, the then U.S. president, George H.W. Bush, had acted on the legal base of an umbrella series of UN Security Council and General Assembly Resolutions, under Chapter VII of the United Nations Charter, directed to rolling-back the Iraqi forces that had invaded Kuwait and to restoring the integrity of Kuwait's territorial frontiers.

A decade later, for purposes of legal control measures to be addressed to the September 11 terrorist attacks, there was an impressive corpus of already existing and only recently adopted international legislation – multilateral treaties, with significant glosses of international administrative cooperative practice built upon them, which were directed specifically to a post-World War II legal plague – aerial piracy. This was the "hijacking" or illegal diversion of commercial civil passenger aircraft while in flight, involving injury to their air crew and passengers and goods, and also attacks on such aircraft and on civil airports and ground installations generally. Any needed ancillary legal remedies in follow-up to the pursuit and punishment of the actual perpetrators, and in retribution against claimed state sponsors of any terrorist organization or cells involved – quickly identified as the Taliban *régime* in Afghanistan – would be obtained, quickly enough, in the full spirit and philosophy of the already existing international anti-terrorist treaties and law, through special, legally enabling Resolutions adopted by the UN Security Council to that end, on the initiative of the US administration and any associated states. This provided the legal base and authority for continuing US and allied actions to apprehend the al-Qaeda leaders, and for the successfully completed military action to defeat and overthrow the

Taliban *régime* in Afghanistan and to replace it by another, claimed politically representative, successor government. The new, post-Taliban government in Afghanistan has been promptly accorded recognition, at the international level, by other states, and has been, equally promptly, seated in the United Nations.

The case for any jump from collective international anti-Terrorist action directed against the al-Qaeda organization and the Taliban *régime* in Afghanistan, to similar collective action against the Saddam Hussein government of Iraq, was not so apparent in political and legal terms. Unless there were to be demonstrated, in clear and unequivocal terms, a direct causal connection between the Iraq government and the al-Qaeda organisation and the Taliban *régime*, legal authority for US and any associated states' action against Iraq would not carry over, automatically, from existing anti-Terrorist International law norms and from the extra legal license specially voted by the UN Security Council in behalf of ancillary military measures in Afghanistan. There might be a case to be made on other, different, political grounds for military intervention against Iraq, but it would have to be argued on its own, separate and distinct merits, such as they might be, and with a different legal rationale invoked to justify any coercive sanctions that might be proposed for that case. It is known, from researches by investigative journalist, Bob Woodward, in a book published in April, 2004, *Plan of Attack*, and confirmed at the time by White House spokesperson Scott McLellan, that President Bush had asked Defence Secretary Rumsfeld as early as November, 2001, to draw up a blueprint for invasion of Iraq. Contingency plans of this sort are the stuff of the war games exercises of most major powers, and do not necessarily imply an actual decision on future action. Nevertheless, it was common belief, in the frenzied rounds of diplomatic negotiations going on from the summer of 2002 to the actual invasion of Iraq in March, 2003, that the US Defence department would have preferred to advance the more frank and straightforward case for producing a *régime* change in Baghdad, rather than to offer the various soft euphemisms that the US administration eventually advanced which rested on assorted factual premises whose truth was easily capable of verification or of rejection: namely, the claimed continued existence in Iraq of Weapons of Mass Destruction (WMD), counter to the Gulf War armistice arrangement of 1991; the further allegation that Iraq was covertly seeking to buy supplies of enriched uranium for use in manufacture of nuclear warheads (a claim later demonstrated to rest on a third party's clumsily forged documents); and even the original claim, counter to all general public knowledge in the World Community at the time, of direct links between the Saddam Hussein *régime* and al-Qaeda and Taliban. The settling on Weapons of Mass Destruction as the official pretext for making war on Iraq seems to have been decided in deference to domestic political sensitivities of British Prime Minister Tony Blair. It was left to US Secretary of State, General Colin Powell, widely respected, outside the US, as a "dove" among the "hawks" in the US administration and as the man who had given the advice, as Commander-in-chief in the Gulf War operations, to halt the allied military onslaught in 1991, for humanitarian reasons, once the originally defined objective of pushing the defeated Iraqi forces in Kuwait back within Iraq's own territorial frontiers had been achieved, to advance in the UN Security Council the obviously painful and difficult case in support of the claimed WMD premise for collective armed action against Iraq. The case, as presented, was not convincing. A joint US/British/Spanish draft Resolution in the Security Council, calling for armed intervention against Iraq, based on historical continuity from the original Security Council and General Assembly legal authority voted in 1990-1 for the then Gulf War operations, signally failed to attract any potential support within the 15-member Security Council, in the February-March, 2002 debates, going beyond its three co-sponsors. It was accordingly allowed to lapse by its three state sponsors.

When the US/British invasion was then launched it was without any fresh, unequivocal United Nations-based legal mandate. It would have to rest, *faute de mieux*, on whatever legal support could be derived, by indirection, from the original Gulf War 1990-1 Resolutions; or from claimed "new" International Law doctrines such as preemptive self-defense or (more daringly still), from even more inchoate legal claims in behalf of a right to intervene for *régime* change.

What we have seen, after the US/British resort to unilateral military action against Iraq, is a clear division of legal opinion as to the present ambit of the UN Charter norms on the Non-Use-of-force and Non-Intervention, and as to the permissible legal limits of the right of self-defense, individual and collective, as set out in Article 51 of the UN Charter.

Once the US/British invasion had begun and the lightning, direct combat side of the operations had been completed by April 15, 2003, an entirely new range of problems began to emerge, not really foreseen by the two invading states in their advance planning, and certainly not fully intended. The classical law on Belligerent Occupation was well enough known in its main principles. But it was not a state-of-war classically defined, that had produced the military defeat and occupation of Iraq. Some of the legal imperfections in the original claim to intervene unilaterally against Iraq, must carry over from that to the legal status of the post-war occupation *régime*. Accepting however, that it was a species of at least *de facto* Belligerent Occupation that one was left with in Iraq after April 15, 2003, with the defeat of the organized armed forces of the government of Iraq, the right/duty legal relationships of the military occupation powers and the defeated people, military and civil, need to be clarified. The more important of the legal questions go to the composition and status of any transitional local *régime* to whom power might eventually be transferred by the occupying powers; to the nature and character of any new, postulated "democratic" constitutional system still to be created in the occupied territories: to the ultimate political configuration and territorial boundaries of the former Iraqi state (whether it is to remain as one state, or to be reconstituted as some form of federal union or association, and whether there are to be territorial readjustments with neighbouring states). A good deal of this remains *terra incognita*, in legal terms, and any ventures take on, necessarily, a sort of law-in-the making dynamic in their own right, with the reaction and legal recognition or non-recognition on the part of other members of the World Community determining constitutional legitimacy and ultimately political viability for any new local *régimes* or state entities that may be created on the initiative of the occupying authority, whether the two invading states or some successor United Nations-based administration.

What became clear, however, once the US administration decided to expand its post-September 11 response from an identification of international terrorism *stricto sensu* and its international legal control, so as to include disposing of unfinished business from the Gulf War, 1990-1, and producing *régime* change in Iraq, was that the problem situation immediately became polycentric in character, dividing into a number of distinct and disparate sub-problems, conveniently separated perhaps by time periods but involving rather difficult legal claims and also, in turn, different legal categorisations and legal remedies.

CHAPTER TWO

INTERNATIONAL LEGAL CONTROLS ON INTERNATIONAL TERRORISM

International terrorism did not begin with the attacks, through the instrument of hijacked commercial passenger aircraft, against the twin World Trade towers in New York City and the Pentagon building in Washington, D.C., on September 11, 2001. It simple re-emerged, with a peculiar immediacy and intensity of agony, because of the spectacular fashion in which the acts of terrorism were achieved and demonstrated to the U.S. and to the World Community at large, through live action, direct televising on the main national and international networks, that was then replayed constantly over the ensuing weeks.

International terrorism had historical roots, for Western societies, in the 19th century anarchist-terrorist movements and political groups or cells whose actions were directed so largely then to the assassination of despotic heads-of-state and their military and civil governors. While the main wave of late 19th and early 20th century anarchism seemed to have occurred in Imperial Russia, with successive Tsars and their police chiefs as the intended targets or victims, few other European states were spared. Successful attacks were achieved against members of other European royal dynastic families (Austro-Hungary (the Empress), Italy, Portugal, Serbia, Greece) and even the heads of liberal republican *régimes* (France, and the US (two Presidents)). It should also to be remembered that World War I was triggered by the assassination, on June 28, 1914, of the Archduke heir to the Austro-Hungarian throne.

In the case of a number of these attacks – the murders of certain of the European dynastic heads – the political motivation was clear. There were also the claims to absence of alternative, effective, more moderate constitutional-legal controls for changing the political system or government. This may account for the degree of political ambivalence and certainly the absence of any substantial pressures for generalised international police controls on the part of leading Western countries. Killing of political tyrants had been sufficiently romanticised in Western European cultural folklore of the period – Schiller's *William Tell* as translated into Rossini's opera, and Sardou's *Tosca* similarly immortalized by Puccini at a later stage, as examples. It helps explain the occasional reticence of some Western states, including the United States, as to applying compulsory extradition, at request of another state, to persons alleged to have committed terrorist crimes of violence against that other state or its officials or public property.

It was not really until the 1930s, with the assassination of the King of Yugoslavia, while on a state visit to France in 1934, and the killing at the same time of the French Foreign Minister who was officially receiving him in Marseilles, that some collective international action occurred. The twin murders were linked to the post-World War I system of military alliances in Central and Eastern Europe, imposed by France and the other military victors on defeated imperial Germany and imperial Austria-Hungary. The alleged assassins were linked to Croatian separatist groups allegedly sponsored by the Mussolini *régime* in Italy. At the French government's initiative, a League of Nations Convention for the Prevention and Punishment of Terrorism was negotiated and drafted and opened for signature in November, 1937, with 24 states opting to sign, most of these the post-Versailles political-military allies of France. The Treaty, in its opening Article, essayed a general definition of "acts of terrorism" as criminal acts directed against a State and intended or calculated to create a state of terror in the minds of particular persons, or a group of persons in the general public.

The Treaty text went on to focus on willful acts causing death or grievous bodily harm or loss of liberty to Heads of State, their designated successors, and their wives and husbands; and also persons charged with public functions when the act was directed against them in their public capacity. There were some ancillary provisions as to willful destruction or damage to public property and endangerment of the lives of members of the public. Although the League of Nations Treaty would have come into legal force after only three state ratifications should be made, in the politically divided climate of the times in the run-up to World War II this minimal number of ratifications was never reached. Although the Soviet Union had signed, Germany, Austria, Hungary, and Italy did not, and neither did Great Britain nor the United States. Of the 24 actual signatories, only one state, India, then part of the *Raj*, bothered to ratify, the ratification being achieved by its then British, imperial rulers. The Treaty was still-born, legally. It seems reasonable to conclude that, apart from the post-Versailles Treaty fissures within Europe itself, the Treaty text's too limited, and highly particularised fixation upon crimes against Heads of State and their immediate families, helps to explain the lack of interest in follow-up on the project on the part of democratic states normally opposed to violence as a means of achieving political ends.

In the early post-World War II period, a new and different form of terrorist began to emerge, responding to the new technology and the opportunities it presented, in comparison to the rather crude techniques of the past which usually involved a lone, bomb-throwing or knife or gun-wielding assailant. This was a new aerial piracy – the hijacking of aircraft as a means of hostage-taking and thereby applying blackmail pressures for political gain. It began, simply enough, with often solo acts by unbalanced individuals or else bandits seeking financial ransoms for the release of the hijacked plane and passengers. These delinquents took advantage of the then absence of adequate security precautions in advance of or during flights. All the publicity resulting from these occasional, isolated acts persuaded terrorist groups as cells organised around particular ideological causes to follow suit, but on an increasingly better disciplined and planned basis. The large policy question in the 1960s was how best to respond to the new terrorist threat in the interest of safeguarding international air transportation and the security of civil passengers and commerce. The major advantage, in planning the best community responses, was that the problem was rooted in a world-wide, well-regulated industry, with significant patterns of cooperation among its constituent members and with agreed, common goals of the freedom of the air and of air transportation of people and goods. The patterns for this had been laid, in contemporary legal terms, in a great multilateral treaty, the Chicago Convention of 1944 which supplemented its basic premise of international cooperation in the air with ample powers as to sanctions where deemed necessary. In addition, there were two great regulatory agencies of a multilateral character, drawing on all main political and ideological systems – the one *public* organisation, the International Civil Aviation Organisation (ICAO), a United Nations specialised agency; and the other private, the International Air Transport Association (IATA), representing in its membership the main national airlines, whether privately owned, as in the West, or publicly owned as in Socialist states. Whatever the *a priori* cultural or ideological differences among these constituent groups' members, they had a common interest in the safety and security of international air transportation and understood the necessity to cooperate among themselves on a basis of full mutuality and reciprocity of interests. The operational methodology for resolving the various problems to the freedom of the air posed by the new aerial piracy suggested itself, logically enough, as one based exclusively on functional efficacy and as therefore sensibly free from the rhetorical name-calling that had distracted some of the earlier Cold War-era diplomatic exchanges on other issues.

The *Institut de Droit International*, which provided such philosophical overview as was needed for the control measures to be adopted, through its 18th Commission (1969-1971) on the Unlawful Diversion of Aircraft, stipulated (in deliberately non-ideological terms) as unlawful under International Law –

> acts of seizure or unauthorised exercise of control of aircraft in flight, jeopardising the life and health of passengers and crew, as well as those of persons on the ground or in other aircraft, in disregard of elementary considerations of humanity.

The *Institut* set the tone for the impressive body of multilateral treaties then emerging on a specific problem-oriented, step-by-step basis in regard to aerial piracy first of all, and later, by logical extension, to other generic issues like the protection of diplomats and the prevention of hostage-taking. The overriding legal principle behind the anti-terrorist controls for these acute contemporary problems:

> . . . no purpose or objective, whether political or other, can constitute justification for such unlawful acts, and . . . every State in whose territory the authors of such acts may be found has the right and the obligation, if it does not extradite such persons, to undertake criminal prosecution against them.

In other words, the legal obligation on every state in its treatment of persons committing proscribed terrorist acts reduces to the categorical rule – *aut dedere, aut judicare.*

It is an international legal principle of hue-and-cry and pursuit and outlawry of offenders, in the postulated interest of the World Community as a whole!

I. International Law-based Responses to the September 11 International Terrorist Attacks*

The legal base for the collective international response to the international terrorist attacks of 11 September 2001, is to be found in the two historically distinct but, in this particular case, converging and mutually complementing, categories of International Law: the *first* involving Chapter VII of the United Nations Charter, providing the legal authority for the use of armed force for the maintenance of international peace and security; and the *second* involving both Customary International Law and also the special group of international treaties interdicting international terrorist activities and establishing international legal controls for that purpose.

---

* Opinion completed and published, March 2002.

II. Use of Armed Force under the United Nations Charter

President George W. Bush, following precedent established by the first President Bush in the Gulf War crisis of 1990-1991, felt able, immediately after the September 11 attacks, to proceed with United Nations authority for military and other control action to be decided upon. The United Nations Security Council adopted, on 12 September 2001, Resolution 1368; and on 28 September 2001, Resolution 1373. Resolution 1368 characterized the September 11 terrorist attacks as a threat to international peace and security, thereby setting the legal foundation for operation of Chapter VII norms (Action with respect to threats to the Peace, Breaches of the Peace, and Acts of Aggression).

As with the collective international response to the Gulf War situation in 1990-1991, where the international forces operated under US military command and under the umbrella legal authority of a detailed series of UN Security Council and General Assembly Resolutions, US-led collective, international armed response to the September 11 international terrorist attacks started out with an unimpeachable source of legal authority. The post-September 11 collective international armed response raises none of the legal doubts and questions that have attended, both before, during and after the particular military operations involved, the NATO military intervention in Kosovo in 1998-9. The NATO military intervention in Kosovo occurred, then, without prior legal authorization by the UN Security Council; or, in default of any Security Council action, by the UN General Assembly on the legal precedent established, in the initiative of President Truman and the US administration, in the Korean War crisis (the Uniting-for-Peace Resolution, Resolution 377A (V), of 3 November 1950, adopted by the UN General Assembly by a vote of 52 to 3, with 2 abstentions).[1]

---

[1] For some authoritative critiques of the legal base offered by the NATO States, see, for example, Kosovo: House of Commons (U.K.) Foreign Affairs Committee 4th Report, June 2002 (including, in particular, the deposition of Professor Ian Brownlie, made at the

III. Individual and Collective Self-Defence

Chapter VII of the UN Charter also recognizes in terms, and thus preserves, the Customary International Law right of self-defence. The last provision in Chapter VII, Article 51, characterizes as an "inherent right" individual or collective self-defence. The right is, however, controlled as to its exercise by limiting conditions set out in Article 51. Its invocation is predicated upon the occurrence of an "armed attack against a Member of the United Nations"; something that, manifestly, was not the case with Kosovo. The right continues in its operations, according again to Article 51, "until the Security Council has taken measures to maintain international peace and security". While it does not require any prior UN authorization and could therefore be called in aid immediately after an armed attack, the right of self-defense is therefore defeasible once the Security Council decides to act. Also, it remains subject to the Customary International Law principles requiring a certain degree of timeliness in the actual response.

Chapter VII action, under Security Council or General Assembly legal aegis, does not suffer from these particular time limitations, though it might require continuing reference back to the original UN mandate to verify the exact ambit and extent of the legal license to use armed force therein granted.

After the effective termination of collective military operations in the Gulf War in 1991 and with an expulsion of the Iraqi invading forces and the restoration of the integrity of Kuwait's territorial frontiers, the military forces of the US and Great Britain continued,

---

invitation of the Foreign Affairs Committee), re-published in 49 ICLQ (2000), 876, 878-905, 905-910; Report of the Standing Senate Committee on Foreign Affairs, Senate of Canada, (Peter Stollery, Chairman), (Ottawa, April 2000); "The new NATO and the evolution of Peacekeeping: implications for Canada"; especially 31-35. For my own analysis, offered at the time, see *The United Nations and a New World Order for a new Millennium: Self-determination, State Succession and Humanitarian Intervention* (2000) 67-72, 72-74.

throughout the decade of the 1990's, sporadic aerial combat operations against Iraq territory and in Iraq territorial air space. The authority for such armed operations was subject to legal question, the explicit legal mandate given by the UN umbrella resolutions adopted in the wake of the Iraqi invasion of Kuwait having, on some views, been exhausted with the successful completion of the roll-back of the Iraqi forces. The obvious political corrective to flaws or gaps in an original UN-derived mandate, of going back to the UN Security Council for a new legal mandate, that would deal, in terms, with any supervening new problems was not pursued by the then US (Clinton) Administration. This may have accounted, in part at least, for the fact that of the thirty-odd states taking part in the original UN authorized collective armed response to the Iraqi invasion of Kuwait, only Great Britain joined with the US in the new, post-cease-fire actions. Having regard to the terms of UN Security Council Resolutions 1368 and 1373 of September, 2001, it would seem sensible for the current US administration to return to the Security Council and to ask for an additional or supplementary legal mandate, if Chapter VII type armed action of the sort applied against Afghanistan is sought to be pursued in the future, against other states identified, euphemistically, as belonging to an "axis of evil" engaged in international terrorist activities.

The spill-over of the legal doubts and questions from the 1998-9 Kosovo operation extends to issues of the legality of the aerial bombardments conducted by the NATO military forces, with loss of life and damage to civilian populations and civilian property and also, incidentally, to foreign diplomatic premises within the targeted areas. The compatibility of the NATO attacks with the 1977 Protocols Additional to the Geneva Conventions of 1949 has been the main question raised, with the complication that even where not specifically adopted and ratified by all individual members of the NATO forces, the 1997 Protocols are normative and legally binding as General Principles of Customary International Law. The legal problem is compounded, in the case of the Kosovo Operation, by the absence of any general legal authority for the NATO operations, as a whole, from the United Nations, in terms of UN Security Council or General

Assembly Resolutions. Would any prior, UN-based general legal authority have been enough, in itself, to dispense legally from compliance with the 1977 Protocols?

The question seems somewhat less complicated in the case of the collective international response to the September 11 terrorist attacks, since there is an unimpeachable UN-based general International Law authority for the response, from the very outset. The answer to the question must be found in the hierarchical relationship, still to be definitively established, between United Nations Charter Law and general International Law (here, specifically, international treaty-based law). An international treaty (at least, if it has not become qualified, itself, as *Jus Cogens*), should sensibly yield to the UN Charter and to decisions of the principal UN organs, the Security Council and the General Assembly, in implementation of, and in accordance with, the Charter. This appears clear from the majority decision of the International Court of Justice in the *Lockerbie* case in 1992, on the application and effect of Article 103 of the UN Charter, which stipulates that, in the event of a conflict between obligations of UN Members under the UN Charter and their obligations under any other international agreement, their obligations under the Charter shall prevail. In the *Lockerbie* case, the International Court in fact ruled, in the course of deciding upon a request for provisional measures, that a Security Council "decision" under Chapter VII of the Charter must prevail over any state obligations under the Montreal Convention of 1971 (on the Suppression of Unlawful Acts against the Safety of Civil Aviation). The International Court decision in *Lockerbie* was the first time in which it had faced the larger, substantive issue of the relation of Charter-based law to general International Law, and the decision was rendered by a divided court (11-to-5 majority); it will no doubt be re-visited in the future by way of further judicial consideration and clarification.[2]

[2] Question of the Interpretation and Application of the 1971 Montreal Convention arising from the Aerial Incident at Lockerbie, Provisional Measures (Libya v. U.K.), ICJ Reports 1992, 3, 15 para. 39; and see also Separate Opinion, Lachs, J. 26-7).

IV. New Anti-Terrorist International Law

Solutions for the legal antinomies or contradictions in the application of UN Charter-based legal norms authorizing and legitimizing the application of armed force against international terrorism seem assisted by the convergence of the special body of International Law on interdiction of international terrorist activities, developed over the past four decades in immediate response to terrorist attacks on the freedom of the air and communications in international civil air transportation. The September 11 international terrorist attacks are, on their uncontested facts, in direct violation of two of the great multilateral conventions developed in that period: the Hague Convention for the Suppression of Unlawful Seizure of Aircraft (signed, 16 December 1970; entered into force, 14 October 1971); and the Montreal Convention for the Suppression of Unlawful Acts against the Safety of Civil Aviation (signed, 23 September 1971; entered into with force, 26 January 1973). The *Institut de Droit International*, in its Resolution adopted at its biennial session in Zagreb in 1971, by a vote of 50 to 0, with 3 abstentions (two of these abstentions turning on a stylistic point of a misplaced comma), completed a résumé of existing International Law *doctrines* on the seizure or unauthorized exercise of control of aircraft in flight. The *Institut* concluded, in its Resolution, that any acts "jeopardizing the life and health of passengers and crew, as well as those of persons on the ground or in other aircraft," are in "disregard of elementary considerations of humanity" and, as such, are unlawful under International Law. In the *Institut*'s restatement of existing International Law, even prior to the entry into legal force of The Hague and the Montreal Conventions, "no purpose or objective, whether political or other, can constitute justification for such unlawful acts, and every state in whose territory authors of such acts may be found has the right and obligation, if it does not extradite such persons, to pursue criminal prosecutions against them".[3]

---

[3] *Annuaire de l'Institut de Droit International*: Report, "*Le détournement illicite des aéronefs*," vol. 54(2), 346-398; 399-403, (1971); and see also, *ibid.*, vol. 54(1), 520-769.

The cumulative effect of Customary International Law and of the special Anti-terrorist, Aerial Piracy multilateral treaties cited is to create an effective legal outlawry of the authors of attacks against civil aircraft and their passengers and aircrew, and an international hue-and-cry against the delinquents involved. *Aut dedere, aut judicare* becomes a mandatory legal obligation cast upon all states to apply direct legal sanctions against the authors of the acts so criminalized. The criminal interdiction in the very sweep and range enters the ranks of imperative principles of International Law – *Jus Cogens.* The criminal interdiction, as it emerges from the *Institut de Droit International*'s Resolution and the two Aerial Piracy Conventions, is comprehensive enough to include in the range of the actors involved, not merely the lower level, in-the-field terrorists, who actually execute the terrorist offences, but also those who devise and plan and authorize it as behind-the-scenes master-minds. As the Soviet jurist, Professor Staroushenko, noted in his presentation to the International Law Association in 1984, "if a State proclaims terrorism as an instrument of its foreign policy, if the governmental authorities get involved in bringing about the criminal acts following, such activities become terrorist activities of a State".[4]

V. International Terrorism and the Law of War *(Jus in Bello)*

Should international terrorism, for the purposes of its legal interdiction and control, be assimilated to the Law of War (*Jus in Bello*)? Beyond that, has such an assimilation already taken place, so that existing legal categories of the Law of War would now pre-empt the special International Law developed, on a consistent but step-by-step basis since World War II, through *doctrines* and *jurisprudence* and state practice and also multilateral conventions and bilateral

---

[4] International Law Association. Paris Reunion. Report (1984), 168-9. Cited in my own monograph, *Aerial Piracy and International Terrorism: the Illegal Diversion of Aircraft and International Law* (2nd rev. ed., 1987); 153, et seq. ("on 'State Terrorism', a latter day legal concept").

treaties and related international instruments. The question has been raised, in particular, as to the applicability of the Geneva Convention of 1949 relative to the Treatment of Prisoners of War (Convention III) to the apprehension by international forces in Afghanistan under US military command, of persons suspected of involvement in the planning or carrying out of the September 11 international terrorist attacks. It should be noted that no legal objections have been advanced to date by the present government of Afghanistan as the state of nationality and *parens patriae*, as such of most of the detainees; nor, apparently, by governments of other states from whom some small number of the detainees might claim nationality or double nationality. There would be some doubt, in any case, of the general applicability of Geneva Convention III of 1949 to this latter group of nationals of "third party" states in view of the supervening changes, in particular, Additional Protocol I, Article 47 (1), developed by the Diplomatic Conference on International Humanitarian Law and opened for signature on 12 December 1977 and entered into force on 7 December 1978. Article 47 (1) was deliberately designed and drafted, at the instance of recently-decolonized Afro-Asian States, to eliminate the problem of foreign freebooters and mercenaries who, as "volunteers", had complicated the problems of post-Imperial succession in the Congo, Angola, and other newly-independent states; and it provides, specifically and in terms, that they "shall not have the right to be a combatant or a prisoner of war."

The better legal opinion would seem to be to recognize that the *Jus in Bello*, with its distinctions between lawful and unlawful combatants and the rights and duties entailed in the status of prisoners of war, has evolved, historically, separately and distinctly from the new International Law on Terrorism. A notable part in the step-by-step evolution of the *Jus in Bello* was played in the late 19th century by the *Institut de Droit International* which moved boldly into the up-dating of the rules of *temperamenta belli*, leading on, eventually, to the initiatives of the two Hague Conventions of 1899 and 1907.[5]

---

[5] See, generally *Annuaire de l'Institut de Droit International*, "Opening Address of President," (biennial reunion, Vancouver), vol. 69 (2002).

The US Military Command for the Afghanistan collective international response, in consultation no doubt with President Bush and the US administration, seems to have moved affirmatively to resolve this particular problem of the choice of the International Law to apply to detainees from the Afghanistan collective international action, by itself according to the detainees many of the same conditions that would be applicable under Geneva Convention III, including provision for regular visitations by International Red Cross representatives and similar officials. This would then accord with the general principles of International Humanitarian Law which, while not conterminous with the Geneva Convention rules, would replicate many of their incidents.

CHAPTER THREE

"ROGUE STATES" AND THE CLAIMED LEGAL DOCTRINE OF PREEMPTIVE STRIKES

President George W. Bush on September 17, 2001, six days after the international terrorist attacks in New York City and Washington D.C., released under the White House seal a collection of assorted addresses the President had given, over the preceding six months, outlining his administration's attempt to define a new approach to the maintenance of international peace and security. The collected speeches were now issued under the comprehensive title, *The National Security Strategy of the United States of America.* The president had earlier, on September 13, 2002, addressed the United Nations General Assembly on the same general theme.

The key paper, in terms of the president's own thinking, is perhaps his address in West Point, New York, on June 1, 2002. After distinguishing the Cold War era, now past, whose then threat, in Bush's words had required the US to "emphasize deterrence of the enemy's use of force" – the "balance of terror" – the president went on to identify what he saw as present deadly challenges to the US coming from "rogue states and terrorists", which he then effectively assimilated.

Among the key characteristics of such "rogue states" in Bush's words: they are "determined to acquire weapons of mass destruction, along with advanced military technology, to be used as threats or offensively to achieve the aggressive designs of these régimes"; they "sponsor terrorism around the globe"; and they "reject basic human values and hate the United States and everything for which it stands".

On the choice of appropriate responses and controls by the US against the danger of attacks by "rogue states": "traditional concepts of deterrence will not work against a terrorist enemy whose armed tactics are wanton destruction and the targeting of innocents", "the United States has long maintained the option of preemptive actions to counter a sufficient threat to our national security. The greater the threat . . . the more compelling the case for taking anticipatory action to defend ourselves, even if uncertainty remains as to the time and place of the enemy's attack. To forestall or prevent such hostile acts by our adversaries, the United States will, if necessary, act preemptively".

As to legal foundations for a new Bush doctrine of a right of preemptive strike, the President suggested: "legal solutions and international jurists often conditioned the legitimacy of preemption on the existence of an imminent threat – most often a visible mobilisation of armies, navies and air forces preparing to attack. We must adapt the concept of imminent threat to the capabilities and objectives of today's adversaries. Rogue states and terrorists do not seek to attack us using conventional means".

It is not clear just which legal scholars and international jurists the president was referring to as supporting the claimed right of preemption. The *Institut de Droit International*, in its Bruges Declaration on the Use of Force, adopted on voice vote on September 2, 2003, and then confirmed by written poll vote of all members, essayed a definitive restatement of the principle of the Non-Use-of-Force in the light of the then still recent US/British invasion of Iraq. The *Institut* decision, by 90 to 15 with 12 abstentions, makes no mention of any right to preemptive strike. Instead, it reaffirms the UN Charter cardinal principle that the threat or use-of-force are prohibited, and that States are bound to settle their disputes by peaceful means; that a war of aggression constitutes an international crime; and that force may be used only in the exercise of the right to legitimate self-defence or with the authorisation of the UN Security Council. The *Institut*, while expressly recalling that the primary responsibility for the maintenance of international peace and security is entrusted to the Security Council, also recognises a potential *rôle* of the UN General Assembly – this on the basis of the 1950 "Uniting for Peace" precedent from the Korean War crisis – to fill any legal gap if the Security Council should become blocked in exercise of its peace-making power by abusive use of the Veto by any one or more Permanent Members of the Council.

The *Institut* Resolution, as declaratory of the existing law, is exhaustive and covers the field. The only possible legal umbrella for any claimed right of preemptive strike would be that right of self-defence, acknowledged in the *Institut* Resolution, in Article 51 of the UN Charter. This right is, however, quite precisely defined and limited under the Charter, as being predicated upon the existence of a prior "armed attack". An Oxford and Harvard educated Australian jurist, and distinguished legal philosopher as well as international lawyer, Julius Stone, had displayed unusual prescience in arguing, in a study published a year before the Cuban Missile Crisis of October, 1962 (Julius Stone, *Quest for Survival. The rôle of Law and Foreign Policy* (1961), p. 47), that in the special conditions of the Cold War and the then existing Bipolar system of World order, a state would not be compelled, literally, to wait until ballistic nuclear weapons were already in place and primed and ready to fire by another state, before taking defensive measures. This was the concept of anticipatory self-defence, to be later advanced by Covey Oliver and others in the special context of the Cuban Missile crisis – a right of anticipatory, collective self-defence for the US and its allies against an imminent threat of emplacement of Soviet Nuclear missiles in Cuban bases, within effective launching range of Washington, D.C., and New York City and key US defence installations. The essential pre-condition for corrective action would, however, be the *imminence* of an attack – literally seconds away; and not some hypothetical future danger, at best long-range in temporal terms. What is clear, in the actual crisis management for the Cuban Missile crisis, as recorded by President Kennedy's legal advisor, Abe Chayes, is that in looking to his available options, President Kennedy deliberately eschewed any temptation to "direct action" outside and also counter to the letter and spirit of the UN Charter, and that he therefore rejected the notion of preemptive strikes against the Soviet missile bases in Cuba. The Kennedy problem-solving in the 1962 crisis remains today as the paradigm for recourse to the "more moderate" controls, not involving the use of armed force, when that will suffice for purposes of countering the perceived threat to the nation. The doctrine of *anticipatory* self-defence, which the Kennedy advisors had linked to Article 51 of that Charter, would provide fully adequate legal justification for the US "quarantine" action against Cuban ports, with the resultant effective embargo on entry of Soviet missile-carrying ships into them.

The few cases, since the entry into force of the United Nations Charter, of unilateral military direct action against another country, without any prior UN authority, turn out, on empirical examination of the factual records, to be either exercises in self-defence in the literal sense as mentioned in classical, customary International Law – as examples, the sometimes successful, special task force unit, rescue missions launched on foreign soil and with or without the consent of the foreign country concerned, designed to liberate the air crew and passengers of hijacked commercial passenger aircraft then being held hostage by the hijackers in that foreign country; or else ventures in Reprisals, a legal claim frequently advanced in the 19th century but severely limited, among other conditions, by the necessity to demonstrate a prior illegal act on the part of the claimed offending state and also proportionality in any response (avoidance of excessive measures out of all proportion to the alleged initial provocation). Reprisals, as a claimed legal doctrine, must be regarded as seriously diminished today with the development of UN Charter law and related doctrines proscribing the recourse to armed force other than with the prior authority of the United Nations itself. For the doctrine of self-defence itself, recognized in terms by the United Nations Charter in Article 51, the celebrated formulation of the conditions for its exercise, advanced by US Secretary of State Daniel Webster in regard to the *Caroline* incident of 1837, remains as authoritative today as it was then: "a necessity of self-defence, instant, overwhelming, leaving no choice of means and no moment for deliberation". The US Secretary of State's addendum thereto, that the response must not be "unreasonable or excessive, since the act justified by the necessity of self-defence must be limited by that necessity and kept clearly within it", would seem even more categorical today, in the light of the UN Charter norms interdicting unilateral recourse to armed force.

I. President Bush and the New U.S. National Security Strategy: the Continuing Relevance of the Legal Adviser and International Law[♦]

President George W. Bush's collection of assorted speeches and other papers outlining his new National Security Strategy,[1] published only four days after his address to the United Nations General Assembly on September 13, 2002, on the same general themes, outlines a new U.S. approach to issues of global peace and security. At the same time it seeks a necessary and overdue liberation of U.S. and allied policy-makers from old policy constructs, which had been developed in the very early days of the Cold War and which had become increasingly dated and a hindrance to clear, rational thinking on foreign policy. It is a new era today in which the old Bipolar structures of World public order, based on a nuclear balance of power between the United States and the Soviet Union, have long since disappeared into the dust-bin of history. The passage from inter-Bloc conflict through Peaceful Co-existence and then *Détente* and eventually on to active cooperation has long since been made, culminating in the final ending of the Cold War itself, symbolized by the fall of the Berlin Wall in 1989.

Containment, as first developed by U.S. State Department expert on the Soviet and Communist World in the earliest post-World War II years, George Kennan, and the later concepts of Mutual Deterrence and Mutual Armed Destruction, perfectly described and justified the key strategic facts of the post-War order for which they were first developed, but they no longer make much sense when projected into the 21st Century, more than a decade after the collapse of the old Soviet Union and after, by all reasonable calculations, the threat of direct nuclear confrontation between the two superpowers of the old Cold War era had disappeared.

♦ Opinion completed and published, October 2002.

1 *The National Security Strategy of the United States of America* (The White House, Washington, D.C., September 17, 2002).

II. The SALT I, ABM Treaty, 1972 Re-visited

President Bush was undoubtedly right, in analytical-legal and also military-strategic terms, when he put aside objections of some more nervous allies and associated states that his Nuclear Missile Defense (NMD) Project, announced shortly after his inauguration in 2001, violated the provisions of the SALT I, ABM Treaty of 1972 and also the nuclear balance of power "ground rules" observed by the two superpowers during the Cold War. As a purely bilateral, Soviet-U.S. accord, the ABM Treaty provided no legal standing or legal interest for any non-signatory states that would give them legal right to complain as to treaty observance or non-observance by the two parties; while Russia, as legal successor to the Soviet Union, raised no formal objection. As for the non-legal, political-strategic issues, again no complaint had been advanced by Russia and this for obvious enough reasons. The original *raison d'être* of the ABM Treaty, for Russia and for the U.S. in their mutual relations, had already disappeared into history, with the end of the Cold War. The new Russia presumably had other, more important, non-military priorities to pursue in its increasingly favourable bilateral relations with the U.S.

History here was repeating itself, after an interval of a decade and a half. In 1986, President Reagan's Legal Advisor, Judge Sofaer, was endeavouring to make spirited public argument, to U.S. allies, to persuade them of the full legal compatibility with the SALT I, ABM Treaty of 1972 of President Reagan's then projected Strategic Defense Initiative (SDI), popularly known as the "Star Wars" project. It was designed to provide a missile-proof screen in outer space.[2] If adopted and made operational, the SDI would certainly have shaken the existing nuclear equilibrium and balance of power between the Soviet Union and the U.S. With public debate outside the U.S. still focused on issues of legal interpretation going to the text of the ABM Treaty and its related documents, the whole legal issue was

---

[2] Discussed in Nagendra Singh and Edward McWhinney, *Nuclear Weapons and Contemporary International Law* (2nd rev. ed., 1989) pp. 329-342, 353-6.

suddenly made dated and largely irrelevant with the resumption by President Gorbachev and President Reagan of the temporarily-stalled East-West *Détente* process, and with the signature, a little over a year later, of the Intermediate-Range and Shorter-Range Missile Treaty (INF) in December, 1987. This was followed in 1989 by the symbolic Fall of the Berlin Wall and by the 1990 Two-plus-Four Treaty (the two Germanies and the four European Occupation powers from World War II) which reunited Germany and ended World War II and the Cold War in the same act.

III. The Legal Basis of the New U.S. National Security Strategy

The legal foundations of the new National Security Strategy have become clearer since the military engagement by the U.S. and its allied and associated states in Afghanistan, and the accompanying, parallel though separate, and still continuing anti-Terrorist operations.

a. *The U.N. Charter and Use-of-Force and Armed Intervention*

It has been clear, from the outset of the Afghanistan military operations, that the prime lesson from the NATO states' armed incursion into Yugoslavia in 1999, with the high-level aerial bombardments that also touched non-military targets (civilians and civilian property, diplomats and diplomatic property), has been learnt. The U.S. Secretary of State in President Clinton's administration, in the political run-up to the 1999 military intervention by the NATO states in Yugoslavia, had reportedly said, when told by the then British Foreign Secretary, Robin Cook, that the lawyers were having difficulty coming up with justifications under the U.N. Charter for the then planned military intervention: "Get new lawyers."[3] In fact, no legal authority

[3] Charles Tiefer (citing Michael Glennon), 96 *American Journal of International Law* 489, at p. 491 (2002).

for the armed intervention was sought or obtained before or during the actual course of the NATO action. One has the impression that the legal advisors were not actively consulted or directly engaged in the crisis-management team for the 1999 Yugoslav operation as they had been, so strikingly in earlier, major U.S. and allied operations during the Cold War period.

b. *Korean Crisis, 1950*

In the Korean Crisis at the opening of the 1950s, U.S. Secretary of State, Dean Acheson, with notable scientific-legal support from Myres McDougal[4] and others, devised the "Uniting for Peace" precedent to meet the threat of a Permanent Member's Veto in the U.N. Security Council. The Uniting for Peace Resolution, adopted by the U.N. General Assembly by a vote of 50 to 5, with 2 abstentions, on November 3, 1950, authorized the General Assembly to fill any gap in the peace-making capacity of the United Nations in situations where "the Security Council because of lack of unanimity of the permanent members, fails to exercise its primary responsibility for the maintenance of international peace and security in any case".

c. *Cuban Missile Crisis, 1962*

In the Cuban Missile Crisis of October, 1962, President Kennedy's Legal Advisor, Abe Chayes, was present throughout the National Security Council's crisis-planning, and his professional-legal advice stands as a paradigm-model for the *rôle* of International Law and the International Lawyer, as jurisconsult, in conflicts resolution. Accepting the hypothesis that the Soviet Union attempt at clandestine emplacement of nuclear missiles in Cuba, with a strike-range capable of reaching Washington, D.C. and beyond, would have upset

[4] M.S. McDougal and R.N. Gardner. "The Veto and the Charter: an interpretation for survival", 60 *Yale Law Journal* 258 (1951); and compare Leo Gross, "Voting in the Security Council: abstention from voting and absence from meetings", *ibid.*, 209.

the existing, Bipolar military-strategic balance, the wise legal counsel was always to escalate slowly in the use of military strike power and in the recourse to armed force, and to employ alternative, more moderate (non-military) controls if these should be sufficient to contain and end the crisis. The naval "Quarantine" measures which President Kennedy actually chose[5] and applied, in rejecting advice from "Hawks" within the National Security Council who preferred direct air strikes against the planned Soviet nuclear missile bases in Cuba, allowed Kennedy's Soviet counterpart, Secretary Khrushchev, to retreat more or less gracefully and in any case without intolerable loss of political face. The peaceful resolution of the Cuban Missile Crisis in October, 1962, was followed ten months later, by the three power (Soviet Union, United States, Great Britain-led) Moscow Test Ban Treaty of August, 1963, the first in what was to become a continuing series of joint Soviet-U.S.-drafted bilateral treaties and also larger, multilateral accords on nuclear and general disarmament – the core of the new International Law of *Détente* and of the pragmatic, empirical, problem-oriented, step-by-step process that was the key to its operational achievement over the next quarter century.

d. *Retrospective Examination of NATO Armed Intervention in Yugoslavia, 1999*

In the few years since the NATO states' armed intervention in Yugoslavia in 1999, there has been considerable retrospective examination of its claimed legal foundations on the part of official, Parliamentary bodies in allied countries, and also private, scientific-legal

[5] A. Chayes, "The Legal Case of U.S. action on Cuba". 47 *Department of State Bulletin* 766 (1962); Chayes, "Law and the Quarantine of Cuba", 41 *Foreign Affairs* 554 (1963); L.C. Meeker, "Defensive Quarantine and the Law", 57 *American Journal of International Law* 515, 523(1963). And see my own contemporaneous study, "The emerging Law of Inter-bloc relations: the October, 1962, crisis as case study", in *'Peaceful Coexistence' and Soviet-Western International Law* (1964), pp. 72-85.

and academic institutions.[6] The mystery still remains as to why a more determined effort was not made to bring the planned operation under the *aegis* of the United Nations and, in particular, under the legal authority of Chapter VII of the U.N. Charter (Action with respect to Threats to the Peace, Breaches of the Peace and Acts of Aggression). This had been the route taken by President George H.W. Bush in the Gulf War of 1990-1, when the U.S. built an alliance of some thirty like-minded states to act in concert to repel the Iraqi forces' armed intervention in Kuwait and then to push back the invaders behind their own frontiers. Operating under the legal umbrella of a series of interlocking Security Council and General Assembly Resolutions, President George H.W. Bush thereby was able to achieve an unimpeachable source of authority in International Law for his own actions and those of the U.S. and Allied armed forces, under Chapter VII of the U.N. Charter.

Why was this approach not followed in relation to the NATO states' armed intervention in Yugoslavia in 1999? It has been suggested that there was a fear of a Permanent Member's Veto in the Security Council on any proposed military action (presumably a veto by Russia or by China, as the only non-NATO states among the five Permanent Members). This hypothesis was never really tested in action, possibly because of failure of diplomacy within the Security Council. In fact, as the NATO high-level aerial bombing campaign proceeded without any immediately conclusive results and with politically embarrassing loss of civilian life and damage to civilian and diplomatic property resulting from the high-level bombing, (what was referred to by NATO officials, euphemistically as "collateral damage") approaches to the Russian government to intervene diplomatically were received positively. The Russian participation was a key to the G-8 Foreign Ministers' meeting at Petersberg on May 6, 1999, which led on to U.N. Security Council

[6] Some of the issues are canvassed in greater detail in my earlier study, *The United Nations and a New World Order for a new Millennium. Self-determination, State Succession and Humanitarian Intervention* (2000).

Resolution 1244 of June 10, 1999 and provided a politically face-saving way of ending the NATO intervention and of reasserting, at the same time, the United Nations' legal authority. Both these legal steps were accomplished in detailed declarations that managed, conspicuously and certainly consciously, to avoid any mention at all of NATO or of the NATO states, as such.

Surprisingly, however, once the original decision had been made to by-pass the Security Council, in terms of seeking its legal authority, under Chapter VII of the Charter, for recourse to armed force and armed intervention, there was the signal failure to proceed by the alternative, U.N. General Assembly-based route, on the "Uniting for Peace" precedent first established in 1950 and repeated on a number of occasions thereafter. One suggested explanation for the omission which applies equally to the decision to by-pass the Security Council, is that the NATO players may have believed that to bring the United Nations in at all would be to subject their planned military operations to U.N supervision and control and thereby to risk some future withdrawal of the U.N. legal authority for a NATO operation that might impact also upon non-military, civilian and other targets, in contravention of the 1977 Protocols Additional to the Geneva Conventions of 1949. A more surprising explanation, which relates specifically to the decision not follow the alternative, U.N. General Assembly-based route to legal authority, is that the NATO players feared that they might not obtain the two-thirds vote in the U.N. General Assembly that would be constitutionally necessary to adopt an authorizing Resolution for an armed intervention, as an "important question" under the U.N. Charter.[7] If that were so, of course, it must surely raise some questions as to the *political* merits of the proposed action, quite apart from any strictly legal questions. There had been enough advance time, in any case – six months or more – to canvass all the legal alternatives in depth and detail, within the governments and Parliamentary assemblies of the key state players. The Canadian government, at the initiative of

---

[7] International Law and Military Law expert, L.C. Green, "The Rule of Law and Human Rights in the Balkans", 37 *Canadian Yearbook of International Law* 223, 244 (1999).

the Government and Opposition parties in the House of Commons, had allowed a special, one-day, non-voting debate in the House on the merits, legal and other, of what was then merely anticipated military action, and this on October 7, 1998, more than five months before the launching of the NATO armed intervention.[8] A further such one-day debate was held on February 17, 1999 – again some weeks *before* the NATO action;[9] with a final debate held on April 12, 1999, three weeks after the commencement of the NATO military action and air strikes.[10]

The likeliest explanation for the failure, by the NATO states, to use at least the alternative, U.N. General Assembly route to legal authority for the proposed armed intervention would seem to be the simplest one: that the non-action in terms of seeking a prior U.N. legal authority was arrived at *per incuriam*. It was a different generation of Foreign Ministers in 1998-9, in comparison to the richly experienced and crisis-tested group of actors who had guided us through the productive years of *Détente* and the end of the Cold War and the resolution, so quickly, of the Gulf War crisis of 1990-1. None of the new class of Foreign Ministers in 1998-9 had been really tested before in situations demanding effective crisis-management and none had been through the fire of direct military service. In comparison to earlier international crisis situations, as in Korea in 1950 and Cuba in October, 1962, they did not seem to have brought the Legal Advisor in to the key deliberations of their crisis planning and management teams. There was certainly no one among the Foreign Ministers with experience in International Law of the caliber, for example, of Dean Acheson in the Korean Crisis of 1950, who would be really capable, on that account, of devising and carrying through a solution that would be legally as well as politically acceptable in World Community terms.

---

[8] *Canada, House of Commons Debate*, vol. 135, no. 134 (1st Session, 36th Parliament).

[9] *Ibid.*, vol. 135, no. 183.

[10] *Ibid.*, vol. 135, no. 205A.

d.i. *Parliamentary Scrutiny*
In the current retrospective examination of the *why* and *how* of the NATO armed intervention in Yugoslavia in 1999, the public enquiries and hearings and deliberations of Parliamentary assemblies stand out.

The United States Senate conducted major debate during the year 2000 (and particularly on May 17-18, 2000, with the debate on the so-called Byrd-Warner Amendment regarding the U.S. *role* in the NATO armed intervention. While a principal focus, in a crucial U.S. Presidential election year, was on the *political* merits of the U.S. involvements in the NATO action – what was described as "Mr. Clinton's War" – there was also significant attention to the International Law questions, including the issue of the legality of the high-level aerial bombardments causing loss of life to civilians and diplomatic personnel, and damage to civilians and diplomatic property.[11]

The British House of Commons, with expert evidence from Professor Ian Brownlie as invited witness, among others, conducted, through its Foreign Affairs Committee, the most concentrated and comprehensive and exhaustive examinations of the legal issues, including the study in depth of the claimed right of Humanitarian Intervention in its historical development, and also treating of particularly interesting ancillary legal points such as the effect of the Vienna Convention on the Law of Treaties on treaties whose conclusion has been procured by coercion of a state through the threat or use of force.[12] The reference, here, was to circumstances surrounding the conclusion of the so-called Rambouillet Accords on Yugoslavia.

Canadian Parliamentary Committees, by comparison, focused principally upon Chapter VII of the U.N. Charter and the legal

---

[11] See, generally, Myron H. Nordquist, "A review of the debate in the United States Senate over the deployment of Ground Troops in Kosovo", *Liber Amicorum Judge Shigeru Oda* (N. Ando, E. McWhinney, R. Wolfrum, eds.) vol. 2 (2002), p. 1555.

[12] *Kosovo: House of Commons (U.K.) Foreign Affairs Committee 4th Report* (June, 2000); re-published in 49 *International and Comparative Law Quarterly* 876, 878-905, 905-910 (2000).

antinomies or contradictions inherent in it; and also, even more specifically, on the process of obtaining legal authority, under Chapter VII, for the use of armed force and for armed intervention. The conclusions and recommendations emerging from the Canadian Senate's Standing Committee on Foreign Affairs are especially clear and categorical:

> That any military operations involving Canada, going beyond the defence of NATO territory, or of Canada's own vital national interests should be authorized by the U.N. Security Council; that if U.N. Security Council authority be not feasible because of application of a Veto, or threat thereof, by a Permanent Member of the Security Council, then the authority of the U.N. General Assembly should be sought on the precedent of the "Uniting for Peace" Resolution adopted by the General Assembly on 3 November, 1950 during the Korean crisis.[13]

In explaining its conclusions and recommendations, the Canadian Senate Committee, echoed opinion expressed by Canadian Parliamentarians themselves during the actual course of the NATO military operations:

> The lack of UN authorization also set an unfortunate precedent. NATO's action in Kosovo could be seen as implying that it can disregard international law when it so chooses. Or, it might lead some to conclude more generally that both individual states and regional organizations may act unilaterally when it serves their purpose.[14]

d.ii. *"Uniting for Peace" Resolution in U.N. General Assembly*
As for the "Uniting for Peace" precedent, providing the alternative, U.N. General Assembly-based route to legal authority for armed

---

[13] *Report of the Standing Senate Committee on Foreign Affairs. Senate of Canada* (Peter Stollery, Chairman), (April, 2000), p. 34.

[14] *Ibid.*, p. 47.

intervention under the United Nations *aegis*, the Canadian Senate Committee had no difficulty in identifying and then listing no less than eight examples of its successful application, after its first invocation in the Korean crisis of 1950 to overcome a potential impasse in the Security Council:[15] Suez, 1956; Hungary, 1956; Lebanon, 1958; Congo, 1960; Bangladesh, 1971; Afghanistan, 1980; the Middle East, 1980; Namibia, 1981.

While the concept of a Humanitarian Intervention had been the first possible legal base advanced in the political run-up in 1998 to the NATO armed intervention of the following year, and while it is certainly canvassed in the several one-day non-voting debates in the Canadian House of Commons preceding the actual military intervention or immediately after that intervention had begun, it had soon become apparent that all the asserted historical precedents for its invocation to justify coercive military action and foreign intervention during the late 19th and early 20th centuries had been, too often, examples of colourable exercises by Imperial, Colonial powers – Great Britain, France, pre-1914 Imperial Germany and the U.S., among others – in pursuit of their own narrow political and invariably economic special interests.

d.iii. *U.N. Charter, Article 51: Self-Defense*

The attention of the Parliamentary Committees turned, logically and inevitably, to Articles 2(4) and 2(7) of the U.N. Charter and their relation to Chapter VII of the Charter, and especially Article 51 on the inherent right of individual or collective self-defense. In this context it would need to be remembered that the very precise restrictions on the recourse to armed force established under the U.N. Charter had been a response in considerable measure to the concerns of the Latin American delegates of the United Nations Founding Conference in San Francisco in the Spring of 1945 which debated and then adopted the new U.N. Charter. These special Latin American concerns flowed from the historical experience of those same states

---

[15] *Ibid.*, p. 33.

with armed intervention, or threats of armed intervention, by the principal Western European and U.S. creditor states to enforce repayment of foreign loans or to guarantee the long-term security of often usurious economic resources concessions to foreign states. Professor Myres McDougal had commented that Article 51 of the Charter in particular, in its "inept language", had as its design:

> only that of accommodating regional organizations, as specifically envisaged for the inter-American system by the Act of Chapultepec, with the more comprehensive, centralized system of collective security projected by the Charter.[16]

The conclusion that emerges from the re-examination, after the event, of the detailed record of inter-governmental diplomatic negotiations and decisions leading up to the NATO states' armed intervention in 1999, must be that the particular route taken – by-passing the United Nations – was politically ill thought-out and unnecessary and legally harmful to the cause of the primacy of the United Nations in international conflicts-resolution.

IV. Use of Armed Force: Continued Relevance of U.N. Security Council and General Assembly

The debate itself has, however, both during and after the 1999 action, had some evident educational value for political leaders in some of the states directly involved. In evidence led to the Canadian House of Commons Foreign Affairs Committee, again *after* the actual event, it was communicated that lawyers in the Canadian armed forces, instructed in International Law, had briefed Canadian military personnel as to legal aspects before each operation in which they were directly involved; and also that Canadian servicemen had not been involved in those of the NATO air strikes that had resulted in loss

---

[16] M.S. McDougal, "The Soviet-Cuban Quarantine and Self-Defense", 57 *American Journal of International Law*, 598, 600 (1963).

of civilian life and in damage to non-military, civilian and diplomatic property.

At the head-of-government level, French President Jacques Chirac and German Chancellor Gerhard Schroeder, at a summit meeting in Hanover on September 8, 2002,[17] indicated categorically that they would not agree to take part in any armed intervention against Iraq without the prior authority of the U.N. Security Council. A similar emerging juridical sensitiveness and awareness on the part of national political leaders was evidenced in the statement by the Canadian Prime Minister, the very next day, that his own government would adopt the same policy.[18]

These public statements of assorted NATO states' political leaders, three years after the 1999 armed intervention, amounted to a sea change in those same states' earlier position and in their decision, then, to by-pass the U.N. Security Council or the General Assembly as to any legal authority on which to base the planned military operation. In these leaders' statements in 2002, there was no accompanying public acknowledgement of any change of position, as such, nor any effort at explanation or rationalization of a *volte face* in legal terms. A timely admission of *mea culpa* – of past error or omission – might have proved more influential or persuasive in inducing leaders of allied states – the U.S. and Great Britain, most notably – in reconsidering their early stated positions on any renewed Iraq operation, in late 2002.

a. *International Law as an Autonomous and Self-Sufficient System*

Does a mature legal system have the obligation to provide a response to every new problem-situation, and a response tailored to the specifications of political leaders seeking to justify a proposed political decision or course of action in legal terms? Abe Chayes who had contributed so significantly to the formulation and execution of

[17] *New York Times* September 9, 2002.

[18] *Globe and Mail* (Toronto), September 10, 2002.

the crisis-control for Cuba in October, 1962, had quoted his colleague, Henry Hart, of the Harvard Law School[19] for the thesis that a legal system, in principle, must be all-embracing, all-pervasive; and that if there is truly, in the mind of the political decision-makers involved, no policy alternative to a suggested cause of action, then a viable legal system must be able to provide satisfying legal support for the proposed action. The Henry Hart proposition is close to the legal fiction of the English Common Law in its historical heyday as being autonomous and self-sufficient, gap-less – and therefore always able to provide a legal formula to cover any new situation. Abe Chayes himself, in the Cuban Missile crisis, in opting for the more moderate legal control of the naval "Quarantine", had provided an imaginative operational synthesis of the Rule of Law internationally and of the needs of *Realpolitik*. In this he had been vindicated historically by the subsequent peaceful resolution of the crisis and by the at least tacit acceptance of his legal formula by the other side.

b. *An Alternative Doctrinal Approach*: Non Liquet

An alternative approach might be to accept that no really adequate or pervasive legal ground or authority had been provided for the NATO armed intervention in 1999 in advance of, or during the actual conduct of the military operations, and then to move on from there. The military actions, having been taken and completed three years ago would now be a problem primarily for the legal historians. The necessary lessons having been drawn from the 1999 exercise, it would now be back to the Security Council and/or General Assembly for any future such initiatives.

Some analogies to this position can be seen in the doctrine, used especially in arbitration decisions, of *Non Liquet*:[20] that one is unable

[19] [1963] *Proceedings of the American Society of International Law*, 10, 11.

[20] Lapradelle-Politis, *Recueil des arbitrages internationaux*, vol. I, p. 398 (*Note*, Asser); W. Wengler, *Völkerrecht*, vol. I (1964), pp. 724, 870. And see generally *Nuclear Weapons (Advisory Opinion)*, ICJ Reports, 1996, 226, *ibid.* 583, (Dissenting Opinion, Higgins, J.); *Haya de la Torre Case*, ICJ Reports 1951, 71.

on the basis of the material in the record, and in the apparent absence of rules of positive law or even general principles of law supporting the legal claim advanced, to render an affirmative decision on the legality of the operation involved.

c. *Afghanistan, 2001-2: U.S. and Allied Return to the Security Council*

That the legal lessons from the 1999 armed intervention, as interpreted in the aftermath by Parliamentary Committees and scientific-legal academies and similar *fora*, had been studied and understood, may be seen perhaps in supervening state practice. President George W. Bush, in responding to the September 11, 2001, international terrorist attacks, while at once invoking Article 51 of the U.N. Charter and the right of self-defence, also went immediately to the Security Council to obtain that additional legal authority for a planned collective military action in Afghanistan that would flow from Security Council supporting Resolutions. In this, he also followed the general precedent and example of President George H.W. Bush in the Gulf War operation of 1990-1, where an unimpeachable source of legal authority for the collective military action to roll back the Iraqi invaders of Kuwait was soon provided by an umbrella group of Security Council and General Assembly Resolution under Chapter VII of the Charter.

d. *Contemporary International Law as to Peace and Security and Use of Armed Force*

In *résumé*, the following propositions seem to emerge as to the contemporary, post-September 11, 2001, International Law as to the maintenance and restoration of international peace and security and the use of armed force under Chapter VII of the Charter:

d.i. *Armed Force, Armed Intervention*

The primary legal base for the use of armed force and armed intervention is provided by a prior, authorizing Resolution of the U.N. Security Council; or in default of Security Council action because of Veto or threat of Veto by a Permanent Member, then by a Resolution of the General Assembly on the "Uniting for Peace" precedent, adopted, as constitutionally required for a General Assembly Resolution on an "important question", by a two-thirds majority vote in the General Assembly.

d.ii. *Self-Defence under the U.N. Charter: Anticipatory Self-Defense*

The inherent right of individual or collective self-defense as recognized in Article 51 of the U.N. Charter, is to be interpreted broadly and should not, in any case, be interpreted so as to exclude, in case of demonstrated clear military necessity, anticipatory self-defense. Quincy Wright had argued, during the Cuban Missile crisis of 1962, that the Article 51 process could not be invoked in support of the "Quarantine" control action since, in effect, the Soviet nuclear missiles had not yet been fired.[21] But the hypothesis of nuclear missiles already primed and ready to be fired and waiting only for the command signal to become operational, had been advanced, with an eerily uncanny foresight, by Julius Stone four years before the actual scenario of the Cuban Missile crisis of October, 1962.[22] Julius Stone's suggested response to the hypothetical question of whether one takes preventive action in that crisis situation was that it would be unreasonable to expect the intended victims to wait before making a riposte, when their own imminent destruction, in a nuclear age, might be only seconds away. Covey Oliver then picked up Stone's prescient argument and advanced a new legal concept, in terms, of "anticipatory, collective self-defence" under Article 51.[23] This for-

---

[21] Quincy Wright, "The Cuban Quarantine", 57 *American Journal of International Law* 546, 559 *et seq.* (1963). Wright's thesis had been fiercely contested, at the time, by other U.S. jurists. See, for example, McDougal, 57 *American Journal of International Law* 597, 599 *et seq.* (1963); W.T. Mallison, Jr., "Limited Naval Blocade or Quarantine-Interdiction: National and Collective Defence Claims valid under International Law", 31 *George Washington Law Review* 335, at 353 *et seq.* (1962); Covey Oliver, "International Law and the Quarantine of Cuba", 57 *American Journal of International Law* 373 (1963).

[22] Julius Stone, *Aggression and World Order* (1958), pp. 99-100.

[23] Oliver, 57 *American Journal of International Law* 373, 375 (1963).

mulation was never contested by the other main protagonist of the time, the Soviet Union, and there seems no reason for going back now. In a more contemporary context, "anticipatory self-defence", if invoked, would remain subject to the limiting conditions established in Article 51, including immediate reporting to the Security Council and then yielding to the Security Council if the Security Council should decide itself to take "measures necessary to maintain international peace and security." Other, more general limiting parameters from customary international law, including the tests of proportionality and of a sufficient contemporaneity of the action complained of and the corrective response, should also apply. Lastly, the *Caroline Case* formulae (*infra*) have an obvious relevance in any *ex post facto* review and evaluation of a corrective response and in any future adjudication of the validity of the invocation of the claim.[24]

d.iii. *Legal Controls for International Terrorism*

The operational separation, for purposes of the collective military action in Afghanistan in 2001-2, between lawful and unlawful combatants, for purposes of application of the *Jus in Bello* and the special protections afforded by the Geneva Convention of 1949 relative to the Treatment of Prisoners of War (Convention III), seems fully justified legally in its exclusion of international terrorists or terrorist groups. The International Law on control of Terrorism developed, historically, separately and distinctly from the Law of War, beginning with the Tokyo, The Hague, and Montreal Conventions (on Aerial Piracy) signed in 1963, 1970 and 1971 respectively and providing their own special legal control measures. Legal protections for persons covered by these and succeeding anti-Terrorist Conventions, would be provided under general International Humanitarian Law, which, in some areas, would replicate protections accorded to prisoners-of-war under the *Jus in Bello*. In regard to

---

[24] See, in this report, the comments by Sienho Yee, *Chinese Journal of International Law* (2002) 292-3.

actual anti-Terrorist controls applied in Afghanistan during the course of the 2001-2 operations, no state appears, in the capacity of *parens patriae*, to have objected to the treatment of its own nationals under these special anti-Terrorist measures.

V. Unilateralism vs. Multilateralism, and the Special Case of Iraq: the Law and Power Antinomy

President George W. Bush, after his conscious decision to return to the Gulf War 1990-1, United Nations-based, Security Council-authorised precedent for the U.S.-led collective armed intervention in Afghanistan in 2001-2, appears to have considered reverting, then, for purposes of any proposed new military intervention in Iraq, to the example of the Clinton administration in going into Yugoslavia in 1999 without any clear and unimpeachable, advance legal mandate from the United Nations. The legal *rationale*, here, would have to be, in the end, that advanced by Dean Acheson in his comments,[25] made immediately after the event, on the legal formulae advanced by then Secretary of State Dean Rusk and Legal Advisor Abe Chayes in justification of the U.S. "Quarantine" action in the Cuban Missile crisis of October 1962. In Dean Acheson's words, there are questions of ultimate power which are beyond the province of law: in effect, *pre*-legal or *meta*-legal questions, like the choice of Austin's sovereign or Kelsen's *Grundnorm*, and it is not the province and function of the International lawyer, *qua* jurist, to purport to rule on these questions. As Dean Acheson saw it, these are "questions of ultimate power – power that comes close to the sources of sovereignty . . . The survival of states is not a matter of law."[26]

This particular formulation comes close to the old historical, and now fairly generally discredited, doctrine of *Staatsraison*. It amounts to an extreme doctrine in legal terms, unless it be qualified by legal

---

[25] Dean Acheson, [1963] *Proceedings of the American Society of International Law* 13.

[26] *Ibid.*, 14.

tests of necessity such as advanced by the U.S. Secretary of State well over a century earlier, in the celebrated *Caroline* case:

> that the threat to national security must be – "instant, overwhelming, leaving no choice of means, and no moment for deliberation"; with the further proviso that the response to the danger must be "limited by that necessity, and kept clearly within it".[27]

The only like situation, encountered throughout the dangerous Cold War years, was perhaps that of the Cuban Missile crisis. In that situation the U.S. administration, with the support of the regional security agency, the Organ-isation of American States, opted to proceed with a prudent economy in the use of power by choosing the alternative, more moderate controls not involving recourse to armed force or, even more, direct nuclear missile strikes; and these controls were judged sufficient to achieve the postulated objectives of removal of the Soviet missiles and missile-launcher installations from Cuba. As the Legal Advisor Abe Chayes, said at the time:

> We were armed necessarily with something more substantial than a lawyer's brief, but though it would not have been enough merely to have the law on our side, it was not irrelevant which side the law was on. The effective deployment of force, the appeal for world support, to say nothing of the ultimate judgement of history, all depend in significant degree on the reality and coherence of the case in law for our action."[28]

Dean Acheson himself, while rejecting any conception of the all-pervasiveness of the present-day international legal system, ended

---

[27] R.Y. Jennings, "The Caroline and McLeod cases". 32 *American Journal of International Law* 82 (1938).

[28] A. Chayes, "Law and the Quarantine of Cuba", 41 *Foreign Affairs* 550 (1963); and see also Chayes, "A Common Lawyer looks at International Law", 78 *Harvard Law Review* 1396 (1965).

up acknowledging the influence of legal principles, in the case of the Cuban Quarantine measures, as "procedural devices designed to reduce the severity of a possible clash."[29] In Dean Acheson's view, "these devices cause wise delay before drastic action, create a 'cooling off' period, permit the consideration of other views".[30]

[29] [1963] *Proceedings of the American Society of International Law*, 13, 14.

[30] *Ibid.*

CHAPTER FOUR

UNILATERALISM VS. MULTILATERALISM: THE UNITED NATIONS CHARTER PROHIBITION ON THE USE-OF-FORCE

The key issues in the, by now, great debate over the legality of the US and British invasion of Iraq on March 20, 2003, and the subsequent long belligerent occupation following on the successful 26-day *Blitzkrieg*, cannot be answered in the abstract. They are crucially dependent, for the ultimate judgement, on the factual record of the events in which they were rooted. The official *casus belli* advanced by US Secretary of State, Colin Powell, in the UN Security Council immediately before the US/British recourse to direct action without prior Security Council authority, was the existence – the continued existence – of Weapons of Mass Destruction in Iraq. This was a question of fact, in the end, for which a politically neutral, third party process was already available in terms of the United Nations monitoring agency UNMOVIC specially created for the purpose, and ready and willing and, (in its own and the evident opinion also of a majority of UN Security Council members), perfectly capable of taking its monitoring mandate to early completion.

An alternative, fall-back pretext for the US/British invasion – advanced as public rationalisation – after the event, that Iraq was a key member of a group of "rogue states" – an "axis of evil" – actively engaged in or committed to Terrorism and terrorist acts against the United States, may have been an inarticulate major premise to direct military action and armed intervention against Iraq from the early days of the Bush administration, even before the September 11, 2001 terrorist attacks. This is a conclusion flowing from the published writings of the former chief anti-Terrorism advisor to the Bush administration, Richard Clarke (in his book, *Against all Enemies. Inside America's War on Terror* (2004)); and, even earlier, from revelations by the former Secretary of the Treasury in the Bush Cabinet, Paul O'Neill (in his book, *The Price of Loyalty*). The rather similar charges advanced by the former Watergate scandals investigatory journalist, Robert Woodward (in his book, *Plan of Attack* (2004)) are more sweeping and also more detailed.

In the case of the WMD pretext, a ready-made, objective third party, UN-based fact-finding process was already in place before the US/British invasion. The question as to the alleged continued existence, within Iraq, of the WMD's was able to be answered, categorically, in Yes or No terms, immediately after the 26-day direct military operations had terminated on April 15, 2003. No WMD's were able to be discovered or produced by the occupying states, then or later.

The alternative, post-invasion legal pretexts – whether the "rogue state" "axis of evil" terrorist characterisation as applied to Iraq; or the further claimed legal justification (relied upon, in particular by the British Prime Minister, Tony Blair) – namely a postulated legal right to armed intervention to produce a *régime* change in the case of a foreign government seen as violating human rights of its own citizens, are all predicated legally upon assertions of fact advanced by the proponent states. In the instant case, these justifications were evidently not accepted uncritically in the World Community, whether by other governments, or by other civil populations, to judge by the size of mass public demonstrations in cities around the World. When the fact-averments by the proponent governments are linked by them to claimed legal remedies, that are, on most counts, novel in International Law terms, and *a fortiori* where those asserted legal remedies are then claimed to be capable of being exercised unilaterally by the moving state or states, the case for leaving any final determination on legal control action to third party, international authority – the United Nations – would seem compelling. Otherwise we are left with a situation where any state, choosing to move unilaterally, would, in effect, be acting as Judge, Jury and Lord High Executioner in its own case.

In the general debate in the *Institut de Droit International* at its

Bruges session, on August 27, 2003, preceding the adoption of its September 2, 2003, declaratory Resolution in Restatement of the contemporary International Law on the Use-of-Force, Ian Brownlie, in commenting on the continuing retrospective review and analysis of the NATO states' armed incursion into Kosovo in the Spring of 1999, highlighted the importance of taking facts into account in assessing the validity of legal claims advanced. Specifically, if one wanted to entertain the proposal that an asserted humanitarian intervention was lawful, one needed to consider whether the practice was authentic. Professor Brownlie cited the example of Lord Robertson who, when he resigned from his position as Minister [of Defence] in the United Kingdom, had produced a pamphlet which was in the public domain and which began with the Dayton Agreements. After those Agreements, NATO "decided to project Western power further into the Balkans." However, only later did Lord Robertson deal with humanitarian intervention. Professor Brownlie then gave a second example in which the OSCE Chairman had sent a circular letter announcing the withdrawal of 1,400 monitors from Kosovo five days before the NATO aerial bombing began. Professor Brownlie concluded with the rhetorical question: Why was this done if there was a humanitarian catastrophe? This practice would have to be looked at and tested.

Public Embarrassment of the respective intelligence services – US and British – on whom the moving governments, arguing for legal authority to intervene unilaterally in Iraq, relied in the UN Security Council debates to support their claim as to the continued existence of WMD's in Iraq, may be partially blunted by the suggestions, in the several national, US and British, investigations after the event and also in the published memoirs and recollections of former officials of both governments, that their intelligence advice as to the facts in issue had been misstated, or misrepresented, or ignored for their own reasons by their elected political superiors. The conclusion emerging inescapably from all this is that for states to act responsibly, in the future, in contested fact-situations on which legal claims involving possible extreme military sanctions depend, they should do so on the basis of an objectively-established, empirically-based factual record. The patient, sometimes viewed as too careful, deliberately non-flamboyant, United Nations special fact-finding agency as to Iraq, UNMOVIC, comes out rather well from the recent international crisis surrounding lead-up to and then the actual decision-making, on the US/British bids for legal authority to invade. It all suggests the merits, long-range, of devising and establishing some more permanent, continuing UN investigatory, monitoring authority for high-level fact-finding assignments for future crisis-situations of similar gravity involving Chapter VII of the UN Charter in the future.

I. The US/British Invasion of Iraq and the United Nations Charter. The Paradox of Unintended Consequences♦

On 20 March 2003 the United States launched an aerial bombardment of Baghdad and the US/British invasion of Iraq had begun.[1] An earlier, joint US/British diplomatic offensive in the United Nations Security Council, with a draft Resolution that would have legally authorized Use-of-Force and armed intervention against Iraq had failed to rally enough advance commitments among Security Council members to secure its adoption if put to a vote. Earlier speculation on a possible veto by one or more of the three remaining Permanent Members (France, Russia, China) in the Security Council had become irrelevant, once it was apparent that the numbers were simply not there to secure passage of the Resolution. In the end, apart from the US and Great Britain, only Spain, which had co-sponsored the US/British draft Resolution, was assured of voting for it in the Council. Equally irrelevant, therefore, was a US/British fail-safe strategy of counting on the "moral" if not legal persuasiveness of a simple majority of the Council in the event of a Permanent Member

♦ Opinion completed and published, August 2003.

[1] Reference generally may be made to the author's earlier study, *The United Nations and a New World Order for a New Millennium. Self-Determination, State Succession, and Humanitarian Intervention* (2000) and see also Anne-Marie Slaughter, *A New World Order* (2004).

veto. The US/British draft Resolution was accordingly withdrawn after a heads-of-government meeting by its three sponsors, held in the Azores on 17 March, had issued a *communiqué* warning President Saddam Hussein of Iraq, in language borrowed from UN Security Council Resolution 1441 of 8 November 2002, of "serious consequences" – amounting euphemistically to a declaration of war against Iraq. The Spanish representative at the Azores meeting had announced, on his return to Madrid, to the applause of deputies in the Spanish legislature, that Spain would contribute no armed forces to the planned military attack on Iraq. Australia and New Zealand had offered logistical support, but for geographical reasons, it was necessarily of a minor or token character. For all practical purposes, the invasion of Iraq reduced to a coalition of the two main "Anglo-Saxon", English-speaking states. One of them, Great Britain, had been the original Imperial, colonial (League of Nations Mandatory) power present at Iraq's creation, after the British and French had divided the spoils of the Ottoman Empire under the Sykes-Picot agreement of 1916 whose terms had been ratified in the post-World War I, Versailles-related treaty settlements of 1919. In contrast, the earlier, US-led Gulf War operation against Iraq, launched by the US President George H.W. Bush under the legal authority of an umbrella series of UN Security Council and General Assembly Resolutions, had managed to enlist a broadly-based, politically-ideologically representative "grand coalition" of 34 states, of which a significant number had offered and delivered direct military-logistical support.

II. From the Gulf War (1990-1) and Afghanistan (2001-2) to the Iraq Invasion: US/British Failure to Produce a Legal Common Front against Iraq

The marked erosion of support, within the United Nations, for US and British enforcement action against Iraq, demonstrated in the swing from 1990-1 to March 2003 in the number of states answering the cry for recourse to armed force and armed intervention, may be explained on a number of different grounds. There seems to have been an over-reaction, within the US administration, to the spontaneous goodwill displayed by so many states, and not merely those in the Western military alliance systems, to the international terrorist attacks against the US of 11 September 2001.

The circumstances, of course, had been somewhat different. The United States was then seen as the victim of internationally lawless acts which potentially threatened all members of the World Community. A common realization of a common threat to the basic fabric of international security had much earlier brought a uniform response – in the 1960s and the 1970s – to international terrorist attacks against the security of civil aviation and the safety of passengers and air crew in international transportation. This had resulted in the three great Aerial Piracy multilateral conventions – Tokyo, The Hague, and Montreal – of that era. This had been followed by similar multilateral conventions directed at protection of heads-of-state and heads-of-government against terrorist attacks and against taking of hostages as instruments in international blackmail and extortion. The legal principle of international outlawry and hue-and-cry against perpetrators of such terrorist attacks, concretized in the obligation imposed on states-signatories – *aut dedere, aut judicare* – was generally accepted in the new, collective international consensus against terrorist activities; and it was a simple generic extension to apply it in late 2001 to those deemed responsible for the September 2001 outrages. The rallying of states to the US cause, with votes in the Security Council for armed action against the apparent sponsors of the September 2001 terrorist acts, the Taliban *régime* of Afghanistan, and also for concrete military assistance to the resulting US operations in the field in Afghanistan, was a logical consequence based on the facts of general public knowledge of the time.

The automatic transference of that same international consensus, from Afghanistan in 2001-2 to Iraq in 2003, was not so apparent. The case would have to be made, and demonstrated on the facts – on an empirically-based record, furnished by independent, professionally expert enquiry. As it happened, two international groups of recognized political integrity and expert status were already available: the United Nations' own specialized agency, the International Atomic Energy Agency (IAEA); and the UN-created special monitoring committee, the UN Monitoring, Verification and Inspection

Committee (UNMOVIC), the latter headed by sometime Swedish Foreign Minister and representative at the UN Headquarters in New York and former head of the IAEA, Hans Blix. In the political maneuvering in the Security Council surrounding the US/British draft Resolution that sought to authorize coercive military action against Iraq, a strong majority of members of the Council were clearly prepared to put their trust in the UN's own specialist investigation committee and to allow it any necessary time to undertake a neutral, scientific enquiry and to report back, before the Council itself should make any decision on whether or not to employ armed force against Iraq.

The political joinder of issue within Security Council ranks thus turned on the fact-finding, as a predicate for any grant of legal authority by the Council. It did not, perhaps, help the US/British draft's chances that a systematic campaign of denigration of Dr. Blix and of his own personal integrity and neutrality and that of his expert committee, seemed to have begun in some US media: Dr. Blix was too well known and respected within the UN extended family of national delegates and permanent diplomatic representatives for any such aspersions to be given too much credence.

It was also a matter of general public knowledge, within the UN, that US and British surveillance and photographic reconnaissance aircraft had been systematically covering Iraq since the termination of Gulf War hostilities in 1991. This had been in purported continuing reliance on the original Gulf War-era Security Council and General Assembly enabling Resolutions, with occasional search and destroy attack missions from military aircraft. Nevertheless, the alarm bells, warranting a renewed invasion of Iraq, had not been rung before. All this would go to the credibility factor, later to become potent, after the termination of hostilities in early April 2003, in terms of general public acceptance, even in the two invading states, the US and Great Britain, of the political wisdom and legal correctness of the decision to invade Iraq, without any prior sanction or legal authority from the Security Council. We have, here, the "*pretext*" issue – the official *casus belli* offered by the US and British administrations in support of their unilateral recourse to armed force and armed interventions in Iraq in March, 2003.

III. The Kosovo, 1999 Precedent: Re-visiting NATO Armed Intervention against Yugoslavia

The intellectual background to the Security Council diplomatic maneuvering and debates in the Fall and Winter, 2002-3, over the US/British plan to go to war against Iraq, had been the continuing sustained and in-depth re-examination in a number of participating states of the legal bases of the NATO states' collective armed intervention against Yugoslavia in 1999, involving high-level aerial bombardments that, inevitably, included non-military, civilian targets in ways outlawed, in terms, under the 1977 Protocols Additional to the Geneva Conventions of 1949. The decision by the US and its European allies in the NATO military alliance to by-pass, in 1999, the United Nations and any legal authority it might have been persuaded to vote in support of such Use of Force and armed intervention, had not needed to be taken overnight, without time or opportunity for consideration and consultation with national legal advisors. There had, in fact, been extensive exchanges between the national foreign ministries involved, over a period of at least six months preceding the first NATO aerial bombardments, as to a possible legal pretext, while at the same time the respective national Parliaments had had the opportunity to debate over the projected operation. In the Canadian Parliament, for example, the potential legal bases offered for an armed intervention had been canvassed in three separate, non-voting debates scheduled in the House of Commons by the government, the first such debate occurring a full six months before the actual NATO military attacks. While it would later be suggested that it was the fear of a Russian or Chinese veto, as Permanent Members of the Security Council, that induced the US and NATO allies to choose to operate outside the United Nations, the issue was never really put to concrete test – either diplomatically in direct, substantive negotiation with Russia and China, or else politically by having a show-down vote in the Council. The question would, in any case, remain if it were fear of an arbitrary or capricious Permanent Member veto in the Security Council, why the US and its European allies did not simply adopt the celebrated Uniting-for-Peace formula – successfully sponsored by US President Harry Truman and his Secretary of State, Dean Acheson, in the Korean crisis of 1950 – of going, instead, to the UN General Assembly for an enabling Resolution to fill any gap in effective application of UN peace-making powers. This would have required, as an "important question" under the UN Charter, a two-thirds majority vote in the General Assembly; but without any right of veto by any state, in contrast to the Security Council. It is difficult to believe that, in choosing not to adopt the Uniting-for-Peace precedent and to take the General Assembly route to legal authority, the US State Department could have been acting *per incuriam*. The better interpretation, in the light of recent publication of the papers of French President François Mitterand,[2] and UN Secretary-General Boutros Boutros-Ghali,[3] would appear to be that casual personalities and clashes of opinion between the US State Department and the United Nations secretariat over most of the 1990s on the sensible conduct of the state succession in International Law to the former Socialist Federal Republic of Yugoslavia – conflicts which brought the US veto of a re-election, to a second term as Secretary General, of Boutros-Ghali when all 14 other members of the Security Council had supported his renewal – lingered on into the late 1990s and dictated an operation free from any United Nations control, even though an apparently more "compatible" successor had emerged by that time in the key post of UN Secretary-General.

In retrospect, revisionist studies of the NATO states' Kosovo operation undertaken by various European governments and legislators

---

[2] Hubert Védrine, *Les mondes de François Mitterand. Á l'Élyseé 1981-1995* (1996).

[3] Boutros Boutros-Ghali, *Unvanquished, A US-UN Saga* (1999). These personality conflicts, within the European alliance and also between the U.S. State Department and the United Nations Secretariat, and their impact on rational policy-formation, are studied more fully in my lectures, "Self-Determination of Peoples and Plural-Ethnic States. Secession and State Sucession and the alternative, federal option". 294 *Recueil des Cours* 167, at 189-90, 205-09 (2003). And see also Madaleine Albright, *Madame Secretary. A Memoir* (2003).

and others, and also by scientific-legal academies like the *Institut de Droit International* whose membership replicates, in many instances, the legal divisions of key national foreign ministries, seem to have been stimulated, politically, by the emergent new fact of "People's Power" as a contributing factor in foreign policy-making at the national level. These had been a negative reaction, in many NATO member-countries, to the observable effects of the NATO states' high-level bombing on civilian targets and civil populations, in apparent contravention of the 1977 Protocols Additional to the Geneva Conventions of 1949 which are explicit in their interdiction of what was identified by NATO command spokespersons, during the course of the 1999 aerial campaign against Yugoslavia, as "collateral" damage.

The most comprehensive of the investigations by national legislators, and certainly the most exhaustive in its analysis and also in the range of jurists invited to testify, is the Report of the Foreign Affairs Committee of the British House of Commons, released in 2000.[4] A quite succinct formulation of issues of law and of constitutional-legal processes in the approach to war is contained in the Report of the Standing Committee on Foreign Affairs of the Canadian Senate, published, like the British House of Commons Committee Report, in the year 2000, three years before the US/British decision to proceed unilaterally, outside the United Nations, with their invasion of Iraq:

> That any military operations involving Canada, going beyond the defence of NATO territory, or of Canada's own vital national interests should be authorized by the U.N. Security Council; that if U.N. Security Council authority be not feasible because of application of a veto, or threat thereof, by a Permanent Member of the Security Council, then the authority of the U.N.

[4] Kosovo: House of Commons (U.K.) Foreign Affairs Committee 4th Report, June 2000 (including, in particular, the deposition of Professor Ian Brownlie made at the invitation of the Committee); republished in 49 ICLQ (2000), 876, 878-905, 905-910.

> General Assembly should be sought on the precedent of the "Uniting for Peace" Resolution adopted by the General Assembly of 3 November 1950 during the Korean Crisis.[5]

In explaining its conclusions and recommendations, the Canadian Senate Committee added:

> The lack of U.N. authorization also set an unfortunate precedent. NATO's action in Kosovo could be seen as implying that it can disregard international law when it so chooses. Or, it might lead some to conclude more generally that both individual states and regional organizations, may act unilaterally when it serves their purpose.[6]

The inarticulate major premise to all revisionist reasoning is that NATO, as a defensive military alliance of Western states of the Cold War era and, as such, a vestigial survival into the post-Cold War era, was not in its historical origins and had never been, a United Nations regional organization for purposes of the UN Charter; and that it could not, therefore, hoist itself by its own bootstraps into a jurisdiction and competence that it did not have under United Nations or general International Law. This might tend to limit the authority of the various condemnations of the claimed legal base for the Kosovo operation to its particular facts of a NATO conceived and directed armed attack and intervention outside the UN Charter. There would be nothing to prevent the consideration, *de novo*, in the larger, United Nations context, of the balance between the UN Charter injunction against the Use-of-Force and armed interventions and potentially countervailing rights and responsibilities of UN member-states under Chapters VI and VII of the Charter as to peace-keeping and peace-making.

---

[5] Report of the Standing Senate Committee on Foreign Affairs, Senate of Canada (Peter Stollery, Chairman), (Ottawa, April 2000), 34.

[6] *Ibid.*, 47.

IV. The UN Security Council and the Iraq Invasion: the "Pretext" Issue

The Security Council debate in February and March, 2003 immediately preceding the US/British invasion, on the possible use of armed force against Iraq, was no emergency response to any suddenly emerging crisis. President George W. Bush, in his address to the Annual Session of the UN General Assembly on 13 September 2002, and his release, four days later, of a collection of assorted, earlier speeches by him, published under the title *The National Security Strategy of the United States of America*, had identified, in terms, as an "Axis of Evil", a number of states that the US administration viewed as inherently dangerous. President Bush had indicated the possibility of preemptive US military strikes against such states if adjudged necessary in the US national interest.

At the same time, the US administration had made substantial new strategic deployment of US military forces in the Middle East region, with significant increases in US land, air, and naval strength in Kuwait and other states adjacent to Iraq.

At the head-of-government level, President Jacques Chirac of France and Chancellor Gerhard Schroeder of Germany, had held a summit meeting in Hanover on 8 September 2002, and had issued a joint declaration that indicated, categorically, that France and Germany would not agree to take part in any armed intervention against Iraq without the prior legal authority of the Security Council in a Security Council Resolution directed to that purpose.[7] The joint French-German declaration was immediately followed, on 9 September 2002, by a statement by the Canadian Prime Minister, Jean Chrétien, that the Canadian government would adopt the same position.[8] This represented a sea change in policy on the Use-of-Force on the part of three major Western states and G-8 members that had been associated with the US in the NATO military inter-

---

[7] *New York Times*, 9 September 2002.

[8] *Globe and Mail* (Toronto), 10 September 2002.

vention against Yugoslavia in 1999, which had by-passed the United Nations. While the revisionist re-examinations of the claimed legal bases of that US-led NATO action of 1999 undoubtedly influenced that change in policy, the actual announcement, in its timing, may have been precipitated by the very sweep and also the uninhibited language of the various public statements by President Bush that became the stuff of the US National Security Strategy booklet released on 17 September 2002. It was evidently to allay fears among some Western allies and associated states of a new US-led Holy War or crusade against "rogue-states" throughout the world that the US administration, on the initiative of Secretary of State Colin Powell, appeared to have opted for a more low-key and certainly lower-decibel strategy limited, for the immediate present, to Iraq, and pursued through the United Nations and UN Charter-based legal processes as the best way of retaining the support of more cautious associated states. General Powell was an excellent choice as the official spokesman for the new, more consciously moderate US approach, having a well-earned reputation, from his Gulf War, 1990-1 military commander-in-chief *rôle*, as someone who understood and practised the principles of economy in the use of power and of defining one's objectives narrowly and always within the limits of what was logistically possible with the resources available for its execution. The UN Security Council then became the arena for a vigorous US diplomatic campaign to secure a majority vote for a UN-authorised, US-led, armed intervention against Iraq. The particular tactic, within the Security Council, of narrowing the political issue to Iraq's alleged violation of its disarmament obligations flowing from the Gulf War cease-fire, reduced to a fact-finding question and judgment; and for that, the United Nations already had its own expert, specialist committee headed by politically independent diplomat-jurist and former head of the UN's Atomic Energy Agency, Hans Blix – *UNMOVIC* – designed for just such a purpose. A hastily prepared technical presentation put together for the most part from British intelligence sources, when presented before the Security Council by Secretary of State, Colin Powell, failed to impress and, more importantly, failed to win over crucial potential votes in the Council. The focus of the Powell brief, echoed with much more rhetorical flair by British Prime Minister Tony Blair and his Foreign Minister Jack Straw, was that Iraq possessed concealed weapons of mass destruction and biological and germ warfare weapons capable (in Prime Minister Blair's phrase) of being launched within 45 minutes. There was the further suggestion that Iraq President Saddam Hussein had been trying to buy enriched uranium from a francophone African State, Niger, and possibly other African states.

Errors or deliberate misstatements or rhetorical exaggerations in claims of this nature were not patent at the time of the Security Council debate, though questioning or doubt, widely held at the time, strengthened the case for taking some more time and leaving it to the UN's already existing monitoring group to investigate and verify. Serious questioning or outright challenge to the pretext advanced for war really emerged only after the termination of direct hostilities in mid-April when, to the evident acute political embarrassment of the invading states and their heads-of-government no weapons of mass destruction and no biological or germ warfare weapons could be found in Iraq. Diplomatic pressures and in particular, economic and financial inducements and offers on pending trade deals, made during the Security Council debate, failed to win over the sought-for votes. Mexico, a partner in the trilateral North American Free Trade Agreement (with the US and Canada), and Chile, the prime candidate for admission to that Agreement and with a pending bilateral trade agreement with the US, were confidently courted but decided against participation in the Iraq operation.

The criticisms, strongly advanced in US media at the time of the Security Council debate, that the United Nations was dysfunctional and incapable of effective operation and should therefore be ignored as irrelevant if it failed to come through with the desired legal approval, proved to be wide of the mark. The Security Council, it may be suggested, functioned in the Iraq case precisely as it had been intended to do, by its Founding Fathers at San Francisco in 1945, in upholding the Charter principle of the non-Use-of-Force and refusing to accept, without the heavy burden of proof on the moving states, the US and Great Britain, having been discharged, that any of the Charter-sanctioned, strictly limited legal exceptions to this principle had been met.

Canada, as a state closely tied historically to the US, with the extra bonds in recent years of the bilateral (Canada-US) Free Trade Agreement and the further trilateral (Canada-US-Mexico) North American Free Trade Agreement, though not currently a member of the Security Council, dissociated itself publicly from the US call for invasion of Iraq. As Prime Minister Jean Chrétien commented, in an address to the US Council on Foreign Relations, in Chicago on 13 February 2003:[9]

> The price of being the World's only superpower is that its motives are sometimes questioned by others. Great strength is not always perceived by others as benign. Not everyone around the world is prepared to take the United States on faith. . . . It is imperative to avoid the perception of a "clash of civilizations". Maximum use of the United Nations will minimize that risk.

Prime Minister Chrétien was equally frank in an interview for the ABC television network that was diffused throughout the United States on 9 March 2003. He rejected the notion that Security Council Resolution 1441 of 9 November 2002 could be invoked as a blanket legal licence from the United Nations to produce a change of *régime* in Iraq:

> Resolution 1441 is about disarmament and . . . it's a question of more days . . . [*Régime* change] is not the debate at the UN . . . China might say, well, we have a problem somewhere

---

[9] The succeeding discussion and citation of Prime Minister Chrétien's statements draws on my guest editorial, The United Nations Charter and the Non-Use-of-Force: the Chrétien Doctrine and the Iraq crisis, 29 *Bulletin of the Canadian Council on International Law*, 1 (2003). The Chrétien Doctrine is further reviewed in my monograph, *Chrétien and Canadian Federalism. Politics and the Constitution, 1993-2003* (2003), at pp. 197, 199-205.

> and you know, we don't like the *régime* and we're going to change the *régime*. It's why it's dangerous. You know, everybody will take that as a pretext.

In answer to a direct question from his US television hosts, in the ABC interview of 9 March 2003 as to whether Canada would fight in Iraq only if there were a UN Resolution authorizing such armed intervention, Prime Minister Chrétien replied:

> It has been the position of Canada since the first day and it was the position of Canada in 1990 [in the Gulf War].

V. After the Iraq Invasion: Charter Legal Principle of the Non-Use-of-Force

The US/British military coalition won its Iraq invasion in a mere 26 days. Winning the peace immediately proved more difficult than winning the war. The victorious coalition seemed unable and ill-prepared to impose an effective belligerent occupation that could, from the outset, re-establish minimum conditions of law and order for the civilian population and also produce a new Iraqi *régime* that could credibly claim to be recognized internationally and to be admitted to Iraq's seat in the United Nations. There was a signal lack of a plan to safeguard the "cradle of civilization" treasures in the National Museum in Baghdad, even though the US Defence department had had a special expert task force that had studied this particular problem in depth, well in advance of the military action. Here what the earlier Greek philosophers had characterized as the paradox of unintended consequences seems to come into play. The invaders were not welcomed, as they had expected, as liberators by any enthusiastic local population. Instead of a quick victory, followed by an equally quick exit strategy – the goal, alike, of effective diplomacy and of military science, it looked like settling into a long occupation, expensive both financially and also in terms of lives of the occupation forces. Having elected to avoid the multilateral approach, through the United Nations and under the political and legal aegis of the United Nations, the two invading states found that other states were not very willing to join in, after the event, to offer to bear part of the huge US and British burden of financial costs, and also costs in human lives, involved in maintaining the occupation of an apparently non-friendly local population. Those few other states that did rally, at least in token form, to the US/British call for material help, as in the case of several former Communist countries of Eastern Europe, had their own political and financial problems and were in evident need themselves of substantial support from outside.

To secure meaningful financial and logistical support from key players in the World Community, it would evidently be useful for the two invading states to at least offer to return the operational control and direction of the Iraq files to the United Nations, so that the post-war reconstruction could henceforth proceed on a genuinely multi-national basis in accordance with the UN Charter. In the absence of such UN legal authority, there remain some very troubling legal problems of the law of belligerent occupation – here *de facto* occupation achieved as a result of a war begun without any legal dispensation from the UN Charter prohibition of the Use-of-Force. Similar legal problems had potentially arisen in the case of the NATO states' armed intervention in Yugoslavia in 1999, also without any prior clear base in International Law. Those problems were sought to be corrected, after the event, through the Petersberg G-8 powers' summit meeting of 6 May 1999 which managed the essential legal transition to UN control within the text of a single succinct communiqué, which was subsequently entrenched in constitutional-legal form in UN Security Resolution 1244 of 10 June 1999. The Security Council Resolution consciously and deliberately avoided any mention of NATO and the NATO states in its short, concise formulation.

The political-legal reality – following the NATO states' intervention in 1999, outside the UN charter, and the subsequent retroactive legal correction – of the necessary continuing vitality of Article 2 (4) of the UN Charter on the Non-Use-of-Force, and the non-licitness of armed interventions without the prior legal authority of the UN Security Council (and, by extension, on the Uniting-for-Peace precedent, of the UN General Assembly in the event of a Veto-imposed deadlock in the Council), is at the core of the Hanover joint declaration of President Chirac and Chancellor Schroeder on 8 September 2002, and adopted the following day by Prime Minister Jean Chrétien. It seems fair to conclude that the same core reasoning also lay behind the decision of the two key Latin-American states, Mexico and Chile in deciding *not* to endorse the US/British draft Resolution of February/March 2003 which had sought Security Council legal authority to make war against Iraq. It was Latin-American states' unhappy historical experiences with armed interventions by the US and also European imperial powers seeking to protect their own economic and political special interests, that had produced the impressive body of Latin-American "regional" International Law *doctrines* from which Article 2 (4) of the UN Charter so largely stemmed.

The now rightly discredited doctrine of "Humanitarian Intervention", which was so often a cloak in time past for Western imperial, colonialist-style adventures, should sensibly yield today, it may be suggested, to the constitutional-legal processes so carefully worked out by the Founding Fathers of the United Nations at San Francisco in 1945, and further elaborated, since then, on a pragmatic, empirical, problem-oriented basis, in subsequent UN practice. If a proposed armed intervention in a claimed crisis or conflict situation cannot meet the constitutional condition of adoption by Security Council vote, or failing that by a two-thirds majority in the General Assembly, it may surely reasonably be questioned as to its substantive political merits.

VI. Continued Multilateral Cooperation in Security Council-Authorized Antiterrorist Action

In spite of the clear political and also doctrinal-level divide over the Iraq invasion in March, 2003, states that have been traditionally associated with the United States, politically and economically and also diplomatically, have maintained their active support and participation, freely pledged in the aftermath of the 11 September 2001 terrorist attacks against the US, to common defense and security operations. The Canadian government, for example, honouring those earlier commitments, announced its replacement, in late 2003, of US Army occupation personnel stationed in Afghanistan, so that the US soldiers could be re-assigned elsewhere and ease US military manpower shortages. Again, Canadian naval forces continued on patrol in the Persian Gulf on reconnaissance/surveillance duties against possible terrorist and arms-smuggling activities, this under the so-called Operation Enduring Freedom introduced after the 11 September attacks. More significantly, politically, perhaps was Prime Minister Chrétien's indication of Canadian support, in principle, for President Bush's Strategic Defense Initiative (SDI) program project as to a missile defense system in space. Prime Minister Chrétien put aside International Law-based complaints as to a possible conflict with the ABM Treaty of 1972. The issue, as with President Reagan's earlier "Star Wars" project, would turn, finally, on economic-financial and not legal considerations.[10] Working cooperation with the US in common anti-terrorist programs would continue without interruption.

VII. Return to Multilateralism? Back to the U.N. and U.N. Charter-based International Law

The difficulties experienced in the immediate post-ceasefire period of Iraq by the two invading states, in reestablishing and maintaining even minimum conditions of public order over a patently unfriendly and uncooperative and frequently hostile local population, have contributed to a timely reconsideration of some originally rigid, *a priori* legal positions advanced in the U.N. Security Council

[10] As to the earlier, comparable legal debate over the Reagan administration's "Star Wars" project, whose demise turned, in the end, as it appears, on financial considerations and not legal ones, see generally Nagendra Singh and McWhinney, *Nuclear Weapons and Contemporary International Law* (1989), at 212, 329-42, 360-3, and 365.

debates of February/March 2003. The effective power vacuum in the larger Mesopotamian region created by the sudden disappearance of the highly centralized Saddam Hussein *régime* destabilized the pre-existing balance-of-power equilibrium of forces painfully achieved, over the years, between Iraq and its immediate neighbours. Putting to one side the *émigré*, exile groups returning in the baggage trains of the invading armies, the evident absence of any credible, indigenous Iraqi political parties able and also ready to fill the gap in internal authority has aggravated long-standing centrifugal, fissiparous tendencies within what had been, in its immediate post-World War I origins, an artificial, ethno-culturally mixed state cobbled together by the original Western European, League of Nations Mandatory power, Great Britain, from three separate and distinct administrative provinces of the then recently defeated Ottoman Empire. Jellinek's celebrated formulation well describes the post-war, "occupation" era situation and the urgent need for corrective action: *die Normative Kraft des Faktischen*. The new fact-situation creates the need for new legal solutions, and also the opportunity for providing such solutions without too many backward glances at past errors or a quest today for attribution of reproach or blame for these errors.

Macro-strategic considerations of this sort and the projection of the dangerous consequences for peace and security and political stability in the Middle East and West Central Asia if the U.S. should become entrapped, long-range, in a Serbonian Bog military occupation adventure from which it could not extricate itself without outside help – diplomatic help, if not yet military-logistical or financial – have produced a disposition to conciliation[11] on the part of the prime supporters of the U.N. *rôle* in the Security Council debates of early 2003. This would be to facilitate any U.S. exit from Iraq without politically-intolerable loss of face – one of the prime lessons from President Kennedy's paradigm approach to resolving the Cuban Missile Crisis of October, 1962.

[11] "Concern over Mideast prompted Europeans to accept U.S. Move" *New York Times*, 17 October, 2003. ("We all see a spiral of violence and terror that is growing in Iraq": Dominique de Villepin, French Foreign Minister, *ibid.*)

On the U.S. side, both the already crushing burden of costs – military-logistical and financial – involved in long-term maintenance of the American military presence in Iraq and, also the already apparent domestic U.S. political reactions to that unexpected burden, seem to have been main catalysts for U.S. diplomatic contact, anew, with those states that had not supported the original U.S.-British resort to unilateral military intervention. The ensuing diplomatic-legal vehicle for this, at least partial, meeting of minds, within the U.N. Security Council has been Security Council Resolution 1511 of 15 October 2003, adopted by unanimous vote of the 15-member Council. The Security Council Resolution does not represent any consensus, at this time, on specific means to be taken immediately to establish United Nations' legal authority and control over the administration of Iraq, and over the military forces presently there. The Resolution constitutes, rather, a principled legal framework on which that result can be approached in the future, pragmatically, on an incremental, step-by-step basis. The prime moving states in the Security Council – France, Germany, Russia and China – might perhaps have preferred a more immediate and complete assertion of United Nations legal authority over conquered Iraq and over a still to be created multilateral occupation military force replacing (though necessarily still including) the two invading states, the U.S. and Great Britain: as well as a precise, unequivocal time-table for restoration of sovereignty to the local, Iraqi population through a credibly representative, elected Iraqi government. However, the general framework principles set out in Resolution 1511 of 15 October 2003 having now been accepted by the current *de facto* occupation powers, normal diplomatic channels remain open to other members of the Security Council and also of the General Assembly, to practise diplomatic persuasion if they wish to ensure the concrete application and further extension of those principles; for example, by exercising the right to condition or withhold their own individual contributions, by way of military-logistical or financial aid,[12] upon continuing

---

[12] "Trio won't contribute troops to Iraq", *New York Times*, 17 October 2003: ("France, Germany and Russia took the unusual step of saying that although they voted for the

demonstrated progress towards fully implementing Resolution 1511, in its spirit as well as in its letter. Reciprocally, the US government as the *de facto* belligerent occupant, might temper its intent to withhold contracts for the rebuilding and reconstruction of Iraq from non-supporting states.

Meanwhile, the debate over the macro-International law issues involved in the U.S.-British invasion of Iraq without prior U.N. Security Council or General Assembly legal license, will proceed in the legal academies, international and national, as well as in national political arenas like the British Government appointed Hutton Commission whose mandate has been to look into the circumstances surrounding the death of Dr. Kelly.[13] This may cover, one may infer, the legal pretext (labeled by the British media as the "dodgy dossier") offered by the British Government in support of the decision to proceed to the unilateral armed intervention in Iraq without prior United Nations legal authority.

The *Institut de Droit International*, in a recent Declaration on the Use of Force (the Bruges Declaration of September 2, 2003), has reaffirmed the primacy in International Law of the U.N. Charter's prohibition on the Use-of-Force, other than where exercised in self-defense under Article 51 of the Charter or where exercised with prior authority of the U.N. Security Council (or the U.N. General Assembly, on the "Uniting-for-Peace" precedent first established in the Korean War Crisis of 1950). The *Institut* Declaration also restates the Classical International Law rules on the legal duties and also legal limitations on the powers of belligerent occupants, whether *de jure* or *de facto*.

---

resolution, they are not happy about it. In a written statement, they said they would not contribute troops to the occupation force and would not boost their financial support for Iraq's reconstruction") *ibid.*

[13] Letter from the Lord Chancellor to Lord Hutton, 24 July, 2003.

CHAPTER FIVE

UNFOLDING OF THE LEGAL DIALECTIC: LEGAL LESSONS FROM SEPTEMBER 11 AND THE IRAQ INVASION

The dialectical character of International law-making through concrete cases and a process of sometimes trial-and-error testing and verification, is well illustrated by the unfolding of legal events, from the September 11, 2001, terrorism attacks, through the US/British invasion of Iraq outside the UN Charter framework and Charter-based norms and processes governing the Use-of-Force, on to the increasingly trouble-plagued military occupation. The US Pragmatist philosopher, John Dewey, in outlining his developmental line of thinking, had much earlier suggested that Truth is not an abstract quality inherent in an idea but something that happens to it, in action, in the contest of people and their ideas. The Protestant theologian, Reinhold Niebuhr, in the same vein, would later reason that Truth sometimes marches into history, on the back of an Error. These are propositions that apply not less to law than to other intellectual disciplines.

I. Law and Fact. The Crucial *Rôle* of Fact-Finding as Premise for Legal Action

The main ground advanced by the sponsors in the Security Council in February-March, 2003, of the US/British/Spanish draft Resolution on Iraq and the US/British invasion that followed on the lapsing of that draft Resolution, was the alleged existence – the continued existence – of Weapons of Mass Destruction in Iraq capable of being made operational virtually immediately. Other ancillary charges raised against the Iraq *régime*, that it was purchasing enriched uranium, for making nuclear warheads, from Francophonic Africa, and that Iraq had direct links to the al-Qaeda terrorist group and to the Taliban *régime* in Afghanistan, were quickly disposed of – the first of these charges as unfounded since based on forged documents, and the second as against all public knowledge in the World Community that Saddam Hussein, whatever other misdeeds he may have committed, ran a determinedly secular state that ruthlessly suppressed and persecuted Shiite religious opponents at home and abroad. On the principal ground, the WMD's, a brave public presentation in the Security Council by Secretary of State, Colin Powell (who, as it now appears, may not himself have been fully persuaded as to his own case), proved unconvincing. A clear majority in the Security Council preferred instead to wait on the report of the special UN agency commissioned to investigate the WMD's issue, *UNMOVIC*, and to allow it enough time to complete its work. After the termination of the lightning war, on April 15, 2003, it soon became apparent, and this to the evident embarrassment of the two invading states, that no WMD's could be found in Iraq. The factual premise on which the case for invasion was based – the pretext for war – had not existed in the first place. Might it not have been wiser, politically and legally, for the two moving states to have based their case for armed intervention frankly and openly on the argument, apparently (according to later published revelations from within the US administration) first canvassed even before the September 11, 2001 terrorist attacks, on the merits of effecting *régime* change in Baghdad? The case could credibly be advanced on the score of Saddam Hussein's *régime* alleged abuses of its own citizens and of regionally-based ethno-cultural and religious communities within Iraq: or else, more nakedly in *Realpolitik* terms, on ensuring continuing access to vital oil resources in the Middle East and West Asia, supposedly under special threat because of the political instability in the area. It is equally likely that, as with the US/British/Spanish draft Resolution in the Security Council that was linked to the WMD's issue, any draft Resolution, grounded in these other terms, would have had difficulty in rallying a clear majority in the

Security Council. But it would at least have had the virtue of candour and of putting the two prime moving states in the vanguard of a campaign, now being sponsored by some Western-based private lobbying groups or NGOs, for the progressive development of classical "New" International law principles postulating a right to intervene in the affairs of another state in protection of human rights in that state. It might also have better safeguarded the international reputation and authority of two great national intelligence and security services that are now being reproached or blamed (possibly unfairly, though the matter is still under public investigation in both states concerned) for the clear factual faults and errors or misinformation now apparent in the briefs relied upon in support of the planned invasion of Iraq. Still later public revelations have suggested that a principal cause of the misinformation or error as to the WMD's may have been emigré/exile Ahmad Chalabi, originally favoured by the US administration to head any new Iraqi government but long removed from the actuality within Iraq.

II. National Decision-Making on War and Peace: Changing Constitutional Balances

The purely military operational side of the Iraq invasion was clearly brilliantly prepared and planned and equally brilliantly executed, in a minimum time and also with minimum casualties to the invading forces. The same can hardly be said for the belligerent occupation that followed on the military victory. There was no comprehensive plan in place for the to-be-expected occupation, involving repair and restoration, by the occupying states, as soon as possible of essential services in the occupied territories (water supplies, electricity, basic communications), provision of food and health services, and maintenance of public order and police security for the civilian population and in regard to civil property. The most surprising, immediate post-victory omission was the signal failure of the occupying powers to protect national archaeological treasures, conveniently located in the national museums in Baghdad, and representing artifacts from the "cradle of civilization" that form part, in United Nations' terms, of the Common Heritage of Humankind.

The lapse, here, seems to have been due to excessive compartmentalization of thinking and planning on the invasion, within the Washington administration, and a failure to separate the problem-situation into its two key components – the military, in the strict sense of the word (where the Defence Department must assume prime control); and the military occupation (where the State Department and other Line Departments in addition to Defence must sensibly work together in what will inevitably progress from the military to mixed military-civil and finally predominantly civil controls).

The paradigm for a successful post-victory occupation of a defeated country with the announced long-range goal of restoring self-government to democratically-elected and constituted local groups with all deliberate speed, must be the remarkably successful US occupations of Germany and Japan after World War II, with their achievement and within a few years only, of model domestic liberal constitutional systems in both countries. There are major political and sociological differences of course between the examples of defeated Germany and Japan on the one hand and defeated Iraq.

But the important first step, in the case of Germany and Japan after World War II, and evidently missing now in relation to Iraq, was several years of intensive advance planning of the Allied Military Government and training of key administrators, both military and civilian, with the organisation ready to be put in place immediately the surrenders of the defeated states had been made. For this objective, the State Department and Defence Department had all worked together in an imaginative cooperative, coordinated plan. One has the impression that the Defence Department, under Secretary Rumsfeld, construed its mandate on Iraq too narrowly, as limited to planning and executing the lightning, low-cost military victory; and that for reasons of inter-Departmental conflicts as to protecting one's own turf or possible personal rivalries between the Department heads concerned, the State Department was not properly engaged in undertaking or sharing the post-victory burden of what became, in fact, a protracted and difficult and dangerous occupation of an increasingly hostile local population. A strong, territorially aggressive head of the National Security Council like Henry Kissinger might have intervened to seize control and supply the necessary coordination of all Cabinet efforts, but the present head, Condoleeza Rice, lacked the obvious political power to try to impose herself in what would have been, in any case, a task rather beyond her presently accumulated professional expertise and inter-personal diplomatic political skills. Vice-President Cheney, who seems to have been the "take-charge" member of the administration on the Iraq files may not have fully appreciated the complex, polycenetic character of the Iraq problem-situation, once the military victory had been gained. It all renders more important than ever the "internationalising" of the occupation in Iraq and the planned transition to a return of self-government to a local *régime* that can command credibility abroad and, more importantly, receive full legal recognition by member-states of the World Community.

III. Legal Adviser, Legal Academies, Private Pressure Groups and NGOs

President Kennedy's successful handling of the Cuban Missile Crisis of October, 1962, is rightly celebrated as paradigm-model for international crisis management in accordance with International Law. The *rôle* of the President's Legal Adviser, Professor Abe Chayes of the Harvard Law School, was clearly crucial in the President's decision-making. Chayes was present, from the very beginning, in all the key Cabinet and National Security Council discussions, and he actively counselled the President, in choosing among his policy-options for conflict-resolution, to prefer the alternative, more moderate controls not involving recourse to armed force, where these more moderate controls would suffice to achieve the desired objectives, and where they would, in any case, in the conscious avoidance of escalation to preemptive military strikes, nuclear or other, as favoured by some "hawks" at the time, be in full accord with accepted legal principles and processes.

Chayes' *rôle*, as Legal Adviser, was no doubt more prominent than is usual in the office. He enjoyed, in addition to the respect for his professional expertise, the full personal confidence of the President and his Secretary of State, Dean Rusk, both of whom accepted the relevance of International Law in the choice among policy alternatives in relation to decision-making.

One has the impression, by comparison, that the *rôle* of the Legal Advisor in the policy-planning in regard to the Iraq invasion and the political lead-up to it was not so pervasive, and that the legal contribution advanced was much more restrained and, by professional choice, more deliberately technical or narrowly professional and not touching the high policy issues between law and politics. In the debates in Great Britain, the co-partner with the US in the Iraq invasion, the public legal defence and justification of the British government's decision to join was entrusted to the Attorney-General, not himself known as an International lawyer, rather than to the professional Legal Advisor.

An increasingly important contribution to the great debate on War and Peace issues, both before and after the Iraq invasion, has been the entry into the dialogue of other, non-governmental actors. As already noted, the *Institut de Droit International*, returning to its classical, late 19th century and early 20th century practice of essaying definitive Restatements or codifications of emerging new International Law on great international tension-issues of the day, adopted at its biennial reunion on September 2, 2003, after spirited discussion and debate within a specialist research Commission and then in plenary session, its Bruges Declaration on the Use of Force and on Belligerent Occupation. The *Institut* decision was later confirmed in written balloting by an overwhelming majority of the Institut's members, fully representative of all main legal systems in the World Community.

There are other, non-academic, private legal actors – the new specialist legal lobbying groups and Non-Governmental Organizations (NGO's) which have contributed disciplined intellectual thinking and some interesting new direction to the International Law debates in various public political and educational arenas. One of the more impressive of these new private legal groups, which was extremely influential in law-making in the decade of the 1990s, was the New York and The Hague-based International Lawyers against Nuclear Arms (*ILANA*), chaired by New York civil rights lawyer, Peter Weis. As a non-profit, largely volunteer association of practising lawyers and legal academics around the World, it successfully spearheaded the initiative in the United Nations in the early 1990s to secure an Advisory Opinion reference to the International Court of Justice on the basic question of the legality, *per se*, of nuclear weapons (including nuclear tests and nuclear proliferation and dissemination necessarily in the larger question). *ILANA*'s initiative included facilitating the intervention in the case, when it was before the World Court, by a number of smaller states not otherwise able to afford expensive litigation in their own right, by having outside counsel prepare the written briefs and appear as counsel for them in the Court hearings, in a *pro bono publico* capacity.

With a proliferation of such private, specialist legal, lobbying pressure groups and NGO's in recent years, some concerns have been raised as to the "interest" base and the sources of their financing and general funding and support, whether governmental or private. Disclosure of just such an interest base, and the political affiliations, covert and otherwise, is an important element in the credibility to be accorded to such groups and to their requests, to Parliamentary and similar assemblies and to the United Nations and related international organizations, to be accorded privileged "expert" status and to be invited to give evidence or to make public depositions before them. These questions could, of course, be easily answered if the public bodies referred to, when receiving requests to be allowed to give expert testimony, would insist, at the preliminary *voir dire* stage, on full disclosure of sources of financing and of the constitution and the membership lists of the lobbying groups or NGO's concerned.

IV. Participatory Democracy: People's Power as Factor in National Decision-Making

The Gulf War, 1990-1, ushered in a new era in policy-making, international and national, on War and Peace issues, by the innovation, through contemporary communication technological advances, of televising live and directly on to family television screens, combat operations while they were actually occurring in the field, before any editing or censorship. CNN, the enterprising new public TV organization, with network links around the world, in producing this veritable revolution in information dissemination, opened up the debate on War and Peace issues to popular participation in a way not seen before. In the developed, post-industrial societies, it coincided with the invention of e-mail and web-sites, and instant access to basic facts and data previously only easily available to political leaders and their advisors and the government bureaucracy as a whole. Even in less developed countries that are as yet without a television screen in every household, images diffused on large community TV screens in village centres – as with the recent, startling, still pictures of treatment of prisoners-of-war in Allied-operated prisons and detention centres – have carried a certain immediacy, and lent power and directness to community anger or sense of outrage.

In Canada, a country that, in the past quarter century, has opened its doors to large-scale immigration outside its traditional historical (English-speaking, French-speaking) sources, the first strong indications of a public desire for participation in key foreign policy decisions emerged with the US-led NATO military intervention in Kosovo in 1999. In the diplomatic run-up to the NATO operation, extending over a period of at least six months preceding the actual attacks, the Canadian government had allowed several non-vote Parliamentary debates on the question of Canada's participation in the NATO operation which considered, among other things the claimed right to exercise a "humanitarian intervention", using armed force, but without any prior legal dispensation by the UN Security Council from the UN Charter prohibitions on the Use-of-Force. These Parliamentary debates were non-determinative on the issue, and in any case, since without any formal House vote, were not binding legally or politically on the government. It was only after the NATO operations had commenced, with the graphic live pictures of what NATO spokespersons referred to as "collateral damage" – direct aerial hits on civilian targets – that a public reaction occurred, particularly strongly at Town Hall meetings attended by recent immigrants from the former constituent republics of the old Socialist Federal Republic of Yugoslavia. The apparent adverse public reaction to the aerial bombardments, carried out in apparent contravention of the 1977 Additional Geneva Protocols concerning aerial bombardment, may have contributed, in part, to Canadian government decisions in regard to the later, 2003 invasion of Iraq, carried out, like the Kosovo operation, without any prior legal dispensation from the UN Charter bans on the recourse to armed force.

The most dramatic evidencing of the new people's power in application to national foreign policy, as influenced by world-wide TV and related direct media coverage, has been seen in the events surrounding the Security Council debates and the US/British invasion of Iraq. The enormous mass meetings and public demonstrations organised in London, Madrid, and Rome and other world cities in opposition to local political leaders' decisions to rally to the US cause, even if (as in Spain and Italy) it was without any contribution of military forces to the actual combat side, were seen and noted around the world and encouraged political questioning in countries, members of the Security Council and also others, still being pressed to make up their minds and to support the armed intervention. Even more dramatic, no doubt, was the decision of the newly elected Social Democratic Premier of Spain, whose party had just defeated that of outgoing Conservative Premier Aznar – who had co-sponsored the US/British draft Resolution in the Security Council, to withdraw all Spanish troops and related personnel from the military occupation forces in Iraq. The new Spanish government's decision to pull out of Iraq occurred in the wake of terrorist attacks, with great loss of civilian life, on Madrid passenger railways; but it had been preceded by public promises by the Socialist party and its leaders, going back almost a year to the Aznar government's original embracing of the US/British intervention, that if elected, they would immediately withdraw Spanish support. In fact, after the new Spanish government announced its decision to withdraw, in April, 2004, a number of other smaller countries (Central American and Caribbean), with very small Occupation contingents in Iraq, announced similar decisions.

V. The Leadership Variable: Changing of the Generations

The 1990s marked a changing of the guard among key political decision-makers in the World Community that has carried over into the first decade of the new century. The post-World War II generation of leaders who had been in power during the Cold War, and who had managed the Cold War's progression into Peaceful Co-existence and active cooperation between the two blocks in problem-solving on key tension-issues of East-West relations, and then, after that, the achievement of *Détente* and finally the ending of the Cold War itself, had given way to a new political *élite* either born after World War II or else too young, as children, to have had any very clear recollections of its horrors. With the close of President Mitterrand's second mandate in 1995, the last of this post-War generation of leaders was gone. It may be noted that the post-War generation, whose character and public personalities were shaped by the wartime experience, consistently displayed an aversion to escalating too early or too quickly to the use of armed force to resolve international conflicts. They understood a prudent economy in the use of power as a principle of diplomacy as much as of War. Thus President Truman (as a World War I combat unit leader), dismissed his Far East Commander-in-Chief, General Douglas MacArthur, when he hazarded extending the Korean conflict into a full-scale war with Communist China in threatening Hot Pursuit of Chinese supporting military forces into Chinese territory. So also President Eisenhower, the World War II Commander-in-Chief, rejected the advice of his civilian Secretary of State, John Foster Dulles, to offer tactical nuclear weapons in aid of the faltering French army in Dienbienphu in 1954. We have already referred to President Kennedy, a World War II combat Naval ensign, and his measured restraint in successful exercise of his policy choices to end the Cuban Missile crisis. President George H.W. Bush, a World War II combat-Naval air arm pilot, directing the Gulf War, United Nations-endorsed collective military action in 1990-1, accepted the advice of then General Colin Powell and stopped the war as soon as the invading Iraqi forces had been pushed out of Kuwait and behind their home frontiers. We know from President Mitterrand's memoirs, as recorded by historian and later Foreign Minister Hubert Védrine, that as a last survivor from the earlier to the new generation of political leaders, his was a cautious, restraining voice in the Balkan conflicts of the 1990's, not always sensibly listened to and heeded in the rush to put aside diplomacy in favour of threat or application of military action. Have the post-post War generation of leaders, without direct personal experience of war, been too ready to escalate into armed confrontation, as a solvent in international relations? The absence of direct combat experience on the part of leaders when of the right military age and when the opportunity was there as during the Vietnam War, has been raised in recent election campaigns in the US, for domestic political purposes. It is not of interest or significance outside US politics, except so far as it may bear on caution or boldness in making the ultimate decision to go to war.

VI. International Decision-Making Arenas: New Political and Constitutional Balances within the United Nations System

During the heated debates in the UN Security Council and with the extreme diplomatic pressures in the corridors, the accusation was occasionally advanced against the United Nations organisation that it is now wholly dysfunctional, and out of touch with present conditions in the World Community and unable to fulfill its original historical mandate for the maintenance of international peace and security. This particular criticism, in retrospect, seems wide of the mark. It was not the decision-making machinery on peace and security, in the United Nations Charter, that was at fault in the failure to carry through to adoption the US/British/Spanish joint draft Resolution on Iraq, but the case for resort to armed intervention as presented by the three moving states which simply failed to convince the other twelve members of the Security Council to whom it was addressed. There was no issue of user – let alone abusive user – of the Permanent Members' right to Veto in the Security Council by any one of the three remaining Permanent Members – France, Russia or China. The draft Resolution could not muster the necessary minimum number of votes (nine out of fifteen) to be able to be adopted, quite apart form the issue of a possible Veto; and this was the reason, in the end, why it was allowed to lapse by its sponsors. The alternative route to adoption of the draft Resolution – in the UN General Assembly on the Uniting-for-Peace formula, originally sponsored by President Truman and Secretary of State, Dean Acheson, in the Korean War crisis in November, 1950 – was not pursued by the three moving states. It would have required, as an "important question" under the UN Charter, a two-thirds majority affirmative vote in the General Assembly for purposes of adoption.

VII. Who Decides on War and Peace, and on When It Is a Just War?

There are strong elements of Natural Law in claims advanced today, predominantly from Western societies, in behalf of an older legal doctrine – up to now generally discredited because of its historical associations with the late 19th century Imperial, Colonial era – of Humanitarian Intervention in the affairs of another state. Those who now propose a revived, contemporary version of the old legal claim, tend to speak of it as a right to protect human rights in another state, whether through collective international action and under a United Nations *aegis*, or through unilateral action on one's own initiative if necessary. It does not necessarily help politically that the proponents of this revived doctrine tend to come from the same Western states historically associated with its abusive use, in the past in its original form, as a cloak for the advancement of the economic and political special interests of the invading power. The real problem is how to decide, on other than a purely subjective basis, whether one is entitled to intervene militarily in another state in exercise of just such a claimed legal right.

If the intervention is to proceed as collective international action, the special machinery and processes applicable in the case of action under Chapter VII of the UN Charter in regard to a "threat to the peace", are ready and available for use: that is to say, a Resolution of the Security Council adopted by a minimum majority of nine out of fifteen states, including the affirmative votes of the five Permanent Members of the Council; or else, in the event of claimed abusive use of a Permanent Member's Veto in the Council, then adopted by a two-thirds majority vote in the General Assembly, on the Uniting-for-Peace precedent. The two, alternative law-making bodies of the United Nations available for invoking such action, the Security Council and the General Assembly, would operate at choice, as a jury of peers assessing the credibility, in factual terms, of the claimed abuse for which a remedy is sought, and could then, if the validity of the claim were accepted, move to legislate and apply appropriate corrective sanctions.

In the absence of such a genuinely international approach to collective action, through the objective constitutional institutions and processes provided under the UN Charter, the problem would seem to remain that any state moving unilaterally, without prior United Nations' legal authority, to intervene in this way would be acting, in effect, as Judge, Jury and Lord High Executioner in its own case, as the sole, self-appointed arbiter on whether it is indeed a "just war"; and whether, in that case, the methods used to vindicate it militarily, in their application to innocent non-combatants, do or do not vitiate any initial claims to justness.

VIII. The United States as Lone Superpower: New Challenges and New Opportunities in the Post-Iraq Invasion Period

The failure of the US/British alliance to rally any really substantial or significant military-logistical support from other states for the actual combat operational phase of the Iraq invasion, was followed by a marked falling away, in the post-victory, belligerent occupation phase, of support, often of a largely symbolic character, thereafter accorded to them by some other states by way of occupation forces and similar personnel. This has induced a re-consideration by the US administration of its original goals and missions in Iraq, and a conclusion that, in the necessary and inevitable progression from a status of belligerent occupation in Iraq to self-government by a constitutionally-selected and fully representative domestic, local administration, it is best and wisest in terms of long-range policy, to internationalise the process by bringing in the United Nations and other appropriate trans-national authority to work with and eventually replace the two invading states. It is an essentially dialectical, trial-and-error, learning process in international law-making, of which perhaps the principal lesson to be learnt is that while one does not really need allies to win a war based on state-of-the art military technology, the arduous, painful task of then winning the peace and restoring law and order in a difficult occupation phase with a non-friendly local population requires a concerted multi-state effort operating under the United Nations or similar international legal auspices and a genuine sharing of the burden, both economic-financial and also the costs in terms of human lives. Excessive reliance on long-absent emigré/exile groups to form a new government, while often providing some rich talent, may not be the best calculated way to improve confidence and support from local populations who have actually lived through and suffered under the former, now-fallen *régime*.

Those states that decided that they could not, compatibly with the primacy they had always accorded historically to the United Nations and to multilateral diplomacy in the determining of the case for applying armed force and armed intervention, join with the United States in the unilateral action, outside the United Nations Charter, in regard to Iraq, have tended, like Canada, to remain steadfast in their original, continuing cooperation and military logistical support, in the international control action against international terrorism, for which an unimpeachable source of legal authority exists under the United Nations Charter and under general International Law. With the United States' commitment, now, to bring in the United Nations in the overseeing and control of the return of self-government in Iraq, this may be the time for a reconsideration of some of the legal objections advanced by the US administration at the time of the original negotiations leading to the adoption of the Rome Statute on the International Criminal Court, and of the Land Mines Treaty. Both of these conventions, because of the US objections at the time and perhaps some extra intransigence on the part of a negotiating majority intent on a complete and perfect final text in spite of the United States, became law without the United States and they are the poorer and less effective in their range and application because of that gap. Pragmatic adjustments, by way of special reservations, or exceptions, to be accepted by other states' signatories to and ratifiers of the Treaty texts – in the one case, of the Rome Treaty, perhaps specifically and in terms exempting from the new Court's jurisdiction actions taken with the United Nations express legal authority under Chapter VII of the UN Charter; and in the other case, the Land Mines Treaty, perhaps exempting the Korean Truce line – now dormant for many years from the range of the Treaty, might succeed in bringing the United States in and signal, symbolically, the general acceptance of a return to Multilateralism again.

US lawyers in their various official and unofficial capacities have undertaken the most extensive public symposium discussions and debates on the legal grounds offered for the invasion of Iraq, and this from a wide variety of scholars expressing frequently widely differing points of view. The American Society of International Law, which is approaching its centennial in the year 2006, has been the principal forum for this internal American debate, through its quarterly law review, the *American Journal of International Law*. The President of the American Society during this testing period, Anne-Marie Slaughter, after offering, in her quarterly Newsletter, early opinions on the legality of the armed invasion predicated upon the factual record as then publicly known, has had the civil courage and intellectual independence to modify those same legal views in her final Newsletter, in the light of the new factual premises now revealed.[1] The same spirit of fidelity to the law is to be seen, throughout the long public debates, in the authoritative *Blue Books* issued by the US Naval War College over the past half-century through its Chair of International Law. For more perhaps than other legal sources, the Blue Books have effectively up-dated the *Jus in Bello* as to Prisoners-of-War and responsibilities and duties of custodial powers under the Geneva Conventions and the Customary International Law rules as *temperamenta belli*, and have been relied on for guidance in the instruction of their own military forces in the application of the Law of War in its important humanitarian aspects, by governments of other countries around the World. They have a special relevance to the anguished public examination by the US administration and by the US Senate and House of Representatives of revelations and charges of abuses to detained civilians and military prisoners long after the termination of the combat operations in Iraq.

[1] Anne-Marie Slaughter, "Reflecting on the War in Iraq One Year Later," *Newsletter American Society of International Law* (March/April 2004) pp. 1-2, 11 replying to William Hartnett, "Relevance and the American Society of International Law", *ibid.*, pp. 1, 11.

APPENDIX

INSTITUT DE DROIT INTERNATIONAL: BRUGES DECLARATION ON THE USE-OF-FORCE AND ON BELLIGERENT OCCUPATION (SEPTEMBER 2, 2003)

The Institut de Droit International, at its 70th biennial reunion held in Bruges, Belgium, in late August/early September 2003, essayed a restatement – styled as the Bruges Declaration – on the Contemporary International Law on the Non-Use-of-Force. The Declaration goes on, beyond that, to provide a timely restatement of the legal responsibilities and also the legal limits of Belligerent Occupation. The *Institut*'s initiative represents a return to its classical, late 19th century and early 20th century *rôle* as private, scientific-legal academy assuming the charge of elaboration and codification of emerging new International Law, with a special concern and mandate for the maintenance of peace and observance of the laws of war.

The Declaration was adopted by the *Institut* in plenary session on the final day of its 70th biennial (Bruges) reunion. The *Institut* decided to submit the declaration to a further, mail-in ballot of all members, so that any not present at Bruges could be included in the result of the final vote. In the result, 90 members of the *Institut* voted in favour of the Declaration, and 15 against, with 12 abstaining. The names of the *Institut* members voting for or against the Declaration, or abstaining, are, according to standard *Institut* practice, recorded publicly.[1]

[1] See Annuaire de l'Institut de Droit International (Session de Bruges), vol. 70 (2004).

The full text of the Bruges Declaration is as follows:

INSTITUT DE DROIT INTERNATIONAL
Bruges Session 2003
BRUGES DECLARATION ON THE USE OF FORCE
2 September 2003
The Institut de Droit International,
Recalls Article 1 of its Statutes adopted by the Ghent International legal conference (*conférence juridique internationale*) of 10 September 1873 in which it is stated that the *Institut*'s

> 2 [. . .] purpose is to promote the progress of international law [. . .] d) by contributing, within the limits of its competence, either to the maintenance of peace, or to the observance of the laws of war.

Recalls its resolution adopted at the Zurich Session in 1877 entitled "Application of the Law of Nations to the War of 1877 between Russia and Turkey" in which it considered itself "unable to close the present Session without again raising its voices in favour of law and humanity".

The *Institut* considers that its duty is to reaffirm that the use of force by States in international relations is governed by international law. One of the major achievements of the twentieth century was the "outlawing" of war, in particular by the Briand-Kellogg Pact whose 75th anniversary is being celebrated, and by the United Nations Charter on the basis of which the following fundamental principles were proclaimed:

- the threat or use of force are prohibited and States are bound to settle their disputes by peaceful means;
- a war of aggression constitutes an international crime;
- force may be used only in the exercise of the right to legitimate self-defence or under the authorization of the Security Council;
- the primary responsibility for the maintenance of international peace and security is entrusted to the Security Council.

Only the Security Council, or the General Assembly acting under the more limited framework of the "Uniting For Peace" Resolution of 1950, may, depending on the particular circumstances at hand, decide that a given situation constitutes a threat to international peace and security, without this necessarily meaning that the recourse to force is the only possible adequate response.

The *Institut* equally reaffirms that acts of terrorism, from whatever source, are prohibited under international law and constitute an international crime.

In addition, the waging of an armed conflict entails the application of the totality of international humanitarian law and in particular, the following principles:

- the distinction between the civilian population and military personnel as well as between civilian objects and military objectives must be respected in all circumstances; and civilian persons and objects must never be targeted;
- combatants who are captured have the right to be treated as prisoners of war; in cases of doubt, their status has to be determined by a tribunal; and even if such a tribunal decides that they do not meet the conditions for the status of prisoner of war, they nonetheless benefit from the rights guaranteed by international humanitarian law in respect of all persons in the power of the enemy (which are codified in Article 75 of the First Additional Protocol of 1977 to the Geneva Convention of 1949).

Belligerent occupation of a territory entails the application of the rules of international humanitarian law codified in the Hague Regulations of 1907, the Fourth Geneva Convention of 1949 and the First Additional Protocol:

- belligerent occupation does not transfer sovereignty over territory to the occupying power;
- the occupying power can only dispose of the resources of the occupied territory to the extent necessary for the current administration of the territory and to meet the essential needs of the population;

- the occupying power assumes the responsibility and the obligation to maintain order and to guarantee the security of the inhabitants of the territory and to protect its historical heritage, cultural property and basic infrastructure essential to the needs of the population;
- the occupying power has the obligation to meet the basic needs of the population;
- the occupying power has the obligation to respect the rights of the inhabitants of the occupied territory which are guaranteed by international humanitarian law and international human rights law, the minimum content of which is codified in Article 75 of the First Additional Protocol.

The *Institut de Droit international* appealing to the universal conscience of mankind, emphatically requests all States to respect the above mentioned fundamental principles.

THE AUTHOR: BIOGRAPHICAL NOTE

Edward Watson McWhinney is a graduate of Yale University, and took his doctorate from Yale (in Constitutional and International Law). He went on to do post-doctoral research work in The Hague, Berlin, Pisa and Geneva.

He was a Lecturer and Assistant Professor at Yale University (in Law and Political Science) for four years, and afterwards held full Chairs at the University of Toronto's Law School and the Centre for Russian Studies; McGill University (where he was also Director of the Air-Space Institute); Indiana University (where he was Director of International and Comparative Law); and most recently, Simon Fraser University in Vancouver. He was named (by special decree of the French Cabinet) Professeur-associé at the University of Paris I (Sorbonne) in 1968, and again in 1982, and 1985. He has been a Visiting Professor teaching at the University of Heidelberg and the Max-Planck-Institut in 1960-61 and 1990, the Meiji University in Tokyo, and The Hague Academy of International Law in 1973, 1990 and 2002. He has also given special courses of lectures at the *Collège de France*; the University of Madrid; the National Autonomous University of Mexico; the Aristotle University of Thessaloniki; the *Institut Universitaire* of Luxemburg; the Institute of Contemporary International Relations in Beijing; and other World centres.

Dr. McWhinney was elected to the *Institut de Droit International* (Geneva), in 1967, the first member elected from Canada to the century and a quarter-old academy. He was elected President of the *Institut* for the two-year term 1999-2001, only the third jurist from outside Europe to be elected to that office.

He was also a Member and Special Advisor of the Canadian delegation to the United Nations General Assembly for three years in the early 1980's.

In his professional life, he has been a Crown Prosecutor; Royal Commissioner of Enquiry; Consultant to the Secretary-General of the United Nations; Constitutional and International Law Advisor to several Quebec Premiers, to the Premier of Ontario, to the federal Government of Canada and to a number of foreign Governments. He was a Member of the Permanent Court of Arbitration, The Hague (1985-1991).

He was elected as the Member of Parliament for Vancouver-Quadra in 1993, and re-elected in 1997, and was successively, Parliamentary Secretary (Fisheries) and Parliamentary Secretary (Foreign Affairs). He chose not to stand for a third term in 2000.

Dr. McWhinney is the author of 26 books (two in French and one in German), and of 14 co-authored books, as well as some 500 scientific articles, published or translated in nine different languages. He is a Past Chairman of the Executive Council of the International Law Association (Canadian Branch), and an Honorary Editor of the *Canadian Yearbook of International Law*.

PUBLICATIONS OF THE AUTHOR

Books as Author

1. *Judicial Review in the English-speaking World* (1st ed., 1956; 4th ed., 1969).
2. *Föderalismus und Bundesverfassungsrecht* (1962).
3. *Constitutionalism in Germany and the Federal Constitutional Court* (1962).
4. *Comparative Federalism. States' Rights and National Power* (1st ed., 1962; ed., 1965).
5. *"Peaceful Coexistence" and Soviet-Western International Law* (1964).
6. *Federal Constitution-Making for a multi-National World* (1966).
7. *International Law and World Revolution* (1967).
8. *Conflit idéologique et Ordre public mondial* (1970).
9. *Parliamentary Privilege and the Publication of Parliamentary Debates* (1974).
10. *The Illegal Diversion of Aircraft and International Law* (1975).
11. *The International Law of Détente. Arms Control, European Security, and East-West Cooperation* (1978).
12. *The World Court and the Contemporary International Law-Making Process* (1979).
13. *Quebec and the Constitution. 1960-1978* (1979).
14. *Conflict and Compromise. International Law and World Order in a Revolutionary Age* (1981).
15. *Constitution-Making. Principles, Process, Practice* (1981).
16. *Canada and the Constitution. 1979-1982. Patriation and the Charter of Rights* (1982).
17. (a) *United Nations Law-Making. Cultural and Ideological Relativism and International Law Making for an Era of Transition* (1984).

(b) French Language Edition: *Les Nations Unies et la Formation du Droit* (1986).

18. *Supreme Courts and Judicial Law Making. Constitutional Tribunals and Constitutional Review* (1986).
19. *Aerial Piracy and International Terrorism* (1987).
20. *The International Court of Justice and Western Tradition of International Law (The Paul Martin Lectures)* (1987).
21. *Nuclear Weapons and Contemporary International Law* (1988) (with President Nagendra Singh).
22. *Judicial Settlement of International Disputes. Jurisdiction, Justiciability and Judicial Law-Making on the Contemporary International Court* (1991).
23. *Judge Shigeru Oda and the Progressive Development of International Law: Opinions on the International Court of Justice, 1976-1992* (1993).
24. *Judge Manfred Lachs and Judicial Law Making: Opinions on the International Court of Justice, 1967-1993* (1995).
25. *The United Nations and a New World Order for a New Millennium. Self-determination, State Succession, and Humanitarian Intervention* (2000).
26. *Chrétien and Canadian Federalism. Politics and the Constitution 1993-2003* (2003).

Books as Joint Author, Editor

1. *Canadian Jurisprudence. The Civil Law and Common Law in Canada* (1958).
2. *Law, Foreign Policy, and the East-West* Détente (1964).
3. *Esquema de un Curso Basico de Derecho Internacional Publico* (1964), with F. Cuevas Cancino, *et al.*
4. *The Freedom of the Air* (1968) (with M.A. Bradley).
5. *New Frontiers in Space Law* (1969) (with M.A. Bradley).
6. *The International Law of Communications* (1970).
7. *Aerial Piracy and International Law* (1971).
8. *Federalism and Supreme Courts and the Integration of Legal Systems* (1973) (with Pierre Pescatore).

9. *La situation de la langue française au Québec* (3 vols.) (1973) (with J.D. Gendron, *et al.*).
10. *Municipal Government in a New Canadian Federal System* (1980).
11. *Mécanismes pour une nouvelle Constitution* (1981) (with Edmond Orban, *et al.*).
12. *From Co-existence to Cooperation. International Law and Organisation in the* post-*Cold War Era* (1991) (with G.I. Tunkin, V.S. Vereshchetin).
13. *Federalism-in-the Making; Contemporary Canadian and German Constitutionalism, National and Transnational* (1992) (with J. Zaslove and W. Wolf).
14. *Liber Amicorum Judge Shigeru Oda* (2 vols.) (2002) (with Nisuke Ando and Rüdiger Wolfrum).

INDEX

NIJHOFF LAW SPECIALS

1. D. Campbell: *Abortion Law and Public Policy.* 1984 ISBN 90-247-3107-0
2. J. Pictet: *Development and Principles of International Humanitarian Law.* 1985 ISBN 90-247-3199-2
3. J. van Houtte: *Sociology of Law and Legal Anthropology in Dutch-speaking Countries.* 1985 ISBN 90-247-3175-5
4. C.D. De Fouloy: *Glossary of NAFTA Terms.* 1994 ISBN 0-7923-2719-5
5. H.L. Zielinski: *Health and Humanitarian Concerns.* Principles and Ethics. 1994 ISBN 0-7923-2963-5
6. K.S. Foster and D.C. Alexander: *Prospects of a US-Chile Free Trade Agreement.* 1994 ISBN 0-7923-2885-X
7. F.J.M. Feldbrugge (ed.): *Russian Federation Legislative Survey.* June 1990-December 1992. 1995 ISBN 0-7923-3243-1
8. R. Platzöder (ed.): *The 1994 United Nations Convention on the Law of the Sea.* Basic Documents with an Introduction. 1995 ISBN 0-7923-3271-7
9. D. Warner (ed.): *New Dimensions of Peacekeeping.* 1995 ISBN 0-7923-3301-2
10. M. van Leeuwen (ed.): *The Future of the International Nuclear Non-Proliferation Regime.* 1995 ISBN 0-7923-3433-7
11. E.-U. Petersmann: *International and European Trade and Environmental Law After the Uruguay Round.* 1995 ISBN 90-411-0857-2
12. V. Gowlland-Debbas: *The Problem of Refugees in the Light of Contemporary International Law Issues.* 1996 ISBN 90-411-0085-7
13. A. Kaczorowska: *International Trade Conventions and Their Effectiveness. Present and Future.* 1995 ISBN 0-7923-3362-4
14. T.F. Acuña: *The United Nations Mission in El Salvador. A Humanitarian Law Perspective.* 1995 ISBN 90-411-0123-3
15. H. Wiggering and A. Sandhövel (eds.): *European Environmental Advisory Councils.* 1996 ISBN 90-411-0873-4
16. E.A. Ankumah: *The African Commission on Human and Peoples' Rights.* Practice and Procedures. 1996 ISBN 90-411-0130-6
17. B. de Rossanet: *Peacemaking and Peacekeeping in Yugoslavia.* 1996 ISBN 90-411-0192-6
18. A. Webster and K. Packer (eds.): *Innovation and the Intellectual Property System.* 1996 ISBN 90-411-0907-2
19. H. Bocken and D. Ryckbost (eds.): *Codification of Environmental Law.* Draft Decree on Environmental Policy. 1996 ISBN 90-411-0911-0
20. K. Lescure and F. Trintignac: *International Justice for Former Yugoslavia.* The Working of the International Criminal Tribunal of the Hague. 1996 ISBN 90-411-0201-9
21. G. de Nooy (ed.): *The Role of European Naval Forces after the Cold War.* 1996 ISBN 90-411-0227-2

NIJHOFF LAW SPECIALS

22. M. Bertrand and D. Warner (eds.): *A New Charter for a Worldwide Organisation?* 1997 ISBN 90-411-0286-8
23. E.-U. Petersmann: *The GATTWTO Dispute Settlement System.* International Law, International Organizations and Dispute Settlement. 1996 ISBN 90-411-0933-1
24. G. de Nooy (ed.): *Cooperative Security, the OSCE, and its Code of Conduct.* 1996 ISBN 90-411-0316-3
25. M. Bertrand: *The United Nations.* Past, Present and Future. 1997 ISBN 90-411-0337-6
26. D. Dijkzeul: *The Management of Multilateral Organizations.* 1997 ISBN 90-411-0356-2
27. G. de Nooy (ed.): *The Role of European Ground and Air Forces after the Cold War.* 1997 ISBN 90-411-0397-X
28. M. Hilaire: *International Law and the United States.* Military Intervention in the Western Hemisphere. 1997 ISBN 90-411-0399-6
29. D. Warner (ed.): *Human Rights and Humanitarian Law.* The Quest for Universality. 1997 ISBN 90-411-0407-0
30. J.C. Hathaway (ed.): *Reconceiving International Refugee Law.* 1997 ISBN 90-411-0418-6
31. G. de Nooy (ed.): *The Clausewitzian Dictum and the Future of Western Military Strategy.* 1997 ISBN 90-411-0455-0
32. Canadian Council on International Law and The Markland Group (ed.): *Treaty Compliance: Some Concerns and Remedies.* 1997 ISBN 90-411-0732-0
33. B. de Rossanet: *War and Peace in the Former Yugoslavia.* 1998 ISBN 90-411-0499-2
34. C.M. Mazzoni (ed.): *A Legal Framework for Bioethics.* 1998 ISBN 90-411-0523-9
35. M. Marín-Bosch: *Votes in the UN General Assembly.* 1998 ISBN 90-411-0564-6
36. L. Caflisch: *The Peaceful Settlement of Disputes between States: Universal and European Perspectives.* Règlement pacifique des différends entre Etats: Perspectives universelle et européenne. 1998 ISBN 90-411-0461-5
37. R. Wazir and N. van Oudenhoven (eds.): *Child Sexual Abuse: What can Governments do?* A Comparative Investigation into Policy Instruments Used in Belgium, Britain, Germany, the Netherlands and Norway. 1998 ISBN 90-411-1034-8
38. E.M. Barron and I. Nielsen (eds.): *Agriculture and Sustainable Land Use in Europe.* 1998 ISBN 90-411-9691-9
39. K. van Walraven (ed.): *Early Warning and Conflict Prevention.* 1998 ISBN 90-411-1064-X
40. S. Shubber: The International Code of Marketing of Breast-milk Substitutes. An International Measure to Protect and Promote Breast-feeding. 1999 ISBN 90-411-1100-X
41. G. Prins and H. Tromp (eds.): *The Future of War.* 2000 ISBN 90-411-1196-4
42. Choung Il Chee: *Korean Perspectives on Ocean Law Issues for the 21st Century.* 2000 ISBN 90-411-1301-0

NIJHOFF LAW SPECIALS

43. K. Idris and M. Bartolo: *A Better United Nations for the New Millennium.* The United Nations System – How it is now and how it should be in the future. 2000 ISBN 90-411-1344-4
44. E. McWhinney: *The United Nations and a New World Order for a New Millennium.* Self-determination, State Succession, and Humanitarian Intervention. 2000 ISBN 90-411-1371-1
45. C.Y. Pak: *Korea and the United Nations.* 2000 ISBN 90-411-1382-7
46. G. Prins and H. Tromp (eds.): *The Future of War.* 2000 ISBN 90-411-1399-1
47. V. Gowlland-Debbas, H. Hadj-Sahraoui and N. Hayashi (eds.): *Multilateral Treaty-making.* The Current Status of Challenges to and Reforms Needed in the International Legislative Process. 2000 ISBN 90-411-1448-3
48. G. Simpson (ed.): *Detainees Denied Justice.* 2001 ISBN 90-411-1552-8
49. C.A. Magariños, G. Assaf, S. Lall, J.D.-Martinussen, R. Ricupero and F. Sercovich: *Reforming the UN System.* UNIDO's Need Driven Model. 2001 ISBN 90-411-1669-9
50. K. Wellens (ed.): *Resolutions and Statements of the United Nations Security Council (1946-2000).* A Thematic Guide. 2001 ISBN 90-411-1722-9
51. P. Soar (ed.): *The New International Directory of Legal Aid.* 2001 ISBN 90-411-1718-0
52. C.M. Mazzoni (ed.): *Ethics and Law in Biological Research.* 2002 ISBN 90-411-1742-3
53. I. Omar: *Emergency Powers and the Courts in India and Pakistan.* 2002 ISBN 90-411-1775-X
54. M. O'Flaherty: *Human Rights and the UN: Practice Before the Treaty Bodies.* 2002 ISBN 90-411-1788-1
55. Y. Beigbeder: *Judging Criminal Leaders.* The Slow Erosion of Impunity. 2002 ISBN 90-411-1815-2
56. Marianne van Leeuwen (ed.): *Confronting Terrorism: European Experiences, Threat Perceptions, and Policies.* 2003 ISBN 90-411-1960-4
57. Ralf Bredel: *Long-term Conflict Prevention and Industrial Development: The United Nations and its Specialized Agency, UNIDO.* 2003 ISBN 90-04-13619-3
58. Raphael Walden: *Racism and Human Rights.* 2004 ISBN 90-04-13651-7
59. Monique Leyenaar: *Political Empowerment of Women: The Netherlands and Other Countries.* 2004 ISBN 90-04-14099-9
60. Sjurdur Skaale (ed.): *The Right to National Self-Determination: The Faroes and Greenland.* 2004 ISBN 90 04 14207 X
61. Edward McWhinney: *The September 11 Terrorist Attacks and the Invasion of Iraq in Contemporary International Law: Opinions on the Emerging New World Order System.* 2004 ISBN 90 04 14143 X

MARTINUS NIJHOFF PUBLISHERS – LEIDEN / BOSTON